P9-DKF-798

**NATIONAL
GEOGRAPHIC
KiDS**

Boredom-BUSTING
Fun Stuff

NATIONAL GEOGRAPHIC
WASHINGTON, D.C.

EXPLORE AWESOME GAMES, JOKES, and MORE FUN!

Get ready to laugh out loud, test your friends, and solve puzzles in this jam-packed book filled with fun activities of all kinds. Whether you're buckling your seat belt for that long road trip, waiting for the bus, or sitting in the comfort of your bed, you're guaranteed to have a blast! Why? Because you, being the fun-loving genius that you are, have picked up this book!

Inside, you'll find hilarious jokes, mind-bending mazes, quizzes to share, and much, much more. Stumped on a game or quiz question? Head to the back to find all the answers!

Just Joking

Sharpen your comedy skills with these sidesplitting knock-knocks, tongue twisters, and more, paired with hilarious animal photography!

Quiz Whiz

From pop culture to history, and all the way to outer space, quiz yourself and your friends on the widest, wackiest, and most exciting array of topics.

Mazes and Search-and-Find

Trek your way through jungles, cities, amusement parks, and more in these games that test your direction and your ability to spot hidden objects and creatures!

4

Signs of the Times

These signs are too outrageous to be real! Or are they? Pick the fakes out of these comical roadside signs. The answers may surprise you.

What in the World?

Some of the most familiar everyday objects look pretty alien up close. Can you tell what they are just by looking at these zoomed-in pictures? Take your best guess!

THE HOLE THING
These photographs show close-up views of things with holes. Unscramble the letters to identify what's in each picture. Bonus: Use the highlighted letters to solve the puzzle below. ANSWERS ON PAGE XXX

GUTONDHU
SISWS ESHECE
TRGAIU

IBRATB LEOH
NERNI EUTB
YEKEOHL

RALCEE
NEMOCBOHY
FOLG OELH

HINT: It's great for a golfer, but not for a pair of pants.
ANWSER: _ _ _ _ O _ _ _ _

Double Take

These two pictures might look the same to you at first.... but take another look and you just might be able to identify the tiny differences.

Hidden Animals

Are your eyes sharp enough to unveil the sneakiest animals' camouflage? See if you can spot the creature hiding in these photos!

Plus more fun games inside!

It's a Jungle Out There!

Help this explorer make her way safely to this tree house. Only one path is danger free!

START

FINISH

DO NOT DISTURB

MAN-EATING PLANTS

DANGER QUICKSAND

SWIM at your OWN RISK

BARREL OF MONKEYS

Just Joking

Sea otter

KNOCK, KNOCK.
Who's there?
Ewan.
Ewan who?
It's just me.

Q How are **two banana peels** like shoes?

A They're a pair of slippers.

TONGUE TWISTER!

Say this fast three times:

Rolling red wagons race wildly down roads.

You've **got** to be joking ...

TWO SNAKES ARE TALKING.

SNAKE 1:
"Are we venomous?"

SNAKE 2:
"Yes, why?"

SNAKE 1:
"I just bit my lip."

To Infinity ...
and Beyond !

1 **When daredevil Felix Baumgartner skydived from the edge of Earth's atmosphere and parachuted back to Earth, about how far did he travel?**

a. 24 miles (39 km)
b. 432 miles (695 km)
c. 5,728 miles (9,218 km)
d. To infinity

2 **How long would it take to get to Mars on a modern spacecraft?**

a. 25 days, if the traffic's not bad
b. 150 to 300 days, depending on how close Earth is to Mars
c. a little over 10 years
d. 23 years, with the right kind of rocket

3 **Which is the farthest distance any human has ever been from Earth?**

a. 6.6 miles (11 km)
b. 23 miles (37 km)
c. 1,324 miles (2,131 km)
d. 248,655 miles (400,171 km)

4 **How many Earths could fit inside Jupiter?**

a. 2
b. 17
c. 200
d. more than 1,000

5 **What travels 186,282 miles (299,792 km) per second?**

a. a comet
b. a spacecraft
c. light
d. an asteroid

6 **What is the record number of days spent in space by a human?**

a. 2
b. 28
c. 438
d. 1,825

7 True or false? Up to 98 percent of astronauts' urine can get recycled back into drinking water on the International Space Station.

8 What is the longest amount of time spent by a human on the moon?

a. 34 minutes
c. about 75 hours
b. 8 hours
d. 5 days

9 How old was the oldest person to ever travel in space?

a. 24 years old
b. 53 years old
c. 77 years old
d. 101 years old

10 About how wide was the asteroid that may have led to the dinosaurs' extinction?

a. as wide as a soccer goal, about 24 feet (7.3 m)
b. as wide as five football fields, about 500 yards (457 m)
c. as wide as 26 Great Pyramids of Egypt, about 6 miles (10 km)
d. as wide as Taiwan, about 106 to 186 miles (171 to 299 km)

11 How long did it take for Apollo 11— the first spacecraft to land on the moon—to reach the moon?

a. 3 days
c. 1 month
b. 1 week
d. 1 year

12 What is the record for the longest human space walk?

a. 32 minutes
b. 8 hours 56 minutes
c. 24 hours
d. 72 hours 45 minutes

Just Joking

Cheetah

KNOCK, KNOCK.
Who's there?
Aardvark.
Aardvark who?
Aardvark a million miles for you!

Q What did the **0** say to the **8**?

A Nice belt.

TONGUE TWISTER!

Say this fast three times:
Shelly is a selfish shellfish.

HA HA HA!

LARRY? ARE YOU IN THERE?

10

Bizarre Buffet

This restaurant's Thanksgiving buffet has gotten a little wacky. Find and circle at least 15 things that are wrong in the scene.

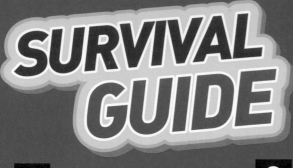

SURVIVAL GUIDE

1 You can survive without water for _____.

a. 3 to 5 days
b. 5 to 7 days
c. 10 days
d. 2 weeks

2 If you have water but no food, you can survive up to _____.

a. 3 days
b. 1 week
c. 3 weeks
d. 8 weeks

3 True or false? Grasshoppers will make a decent meal for a hungry person.

4 Which tool would be *most* useful if you were lost in the woods for a while?

a. an oven mitt
b. a water purifier
c. a comic book
d. toilet paper

5 True or false? If you have frostbitten toes, you should warm them by rubbing them.

6 What should you do if you get separated from your hiking buddies?

a. Stay put and signal for help.
b. Immediately set up a tent.
c. Do nothing.
d. Change into warmer clothes.

7 If you come across a bear in the woods, you should _____.

a. drop down to the ground
b. climb a tree
c. make lots of noise to scare it away
d. feed the bear

8 True or false? If you are stuck in the wilderness, you should never eat the bark of pine trees.

9 What should you do if you come across a swarm of wasps in the woods?

a. Run away fast.
b. Dig a hole in the ground.
c. Jump in a pond.
d. Hide in a tree.

10 True or false? A T-shirt is an excellent tool for catching fish.

11 What is the best way to travel in the woods?

a. with a group
b. with no gear
c. during severe weather
d. in the middle of the night

12 Which of these ingredients should *not* be added to a cookout stew because it is poisonous?

a. fish
b. yew berry
c. grasshopper
d. grub

13 Which edible water plant is known as the "supermarket of the swamp" because different parts of it can be eaten all year long?

a. cattail
b. lily pad
c. algae
d. watercress

14 Which household object could help you catch food if you were lost in the wilderness?

a. dental floss
b. a paper towel
c. shoe polish
d. a flashlight

ANiMaL JaM

Treasure Hunt

The *Animal Jam* characters found an old treasure map, but a maze stands between them and their riches. Help them find their way through Jamaa to the treasure.

BONUS: Find ten gems hidden in the maze's paths.

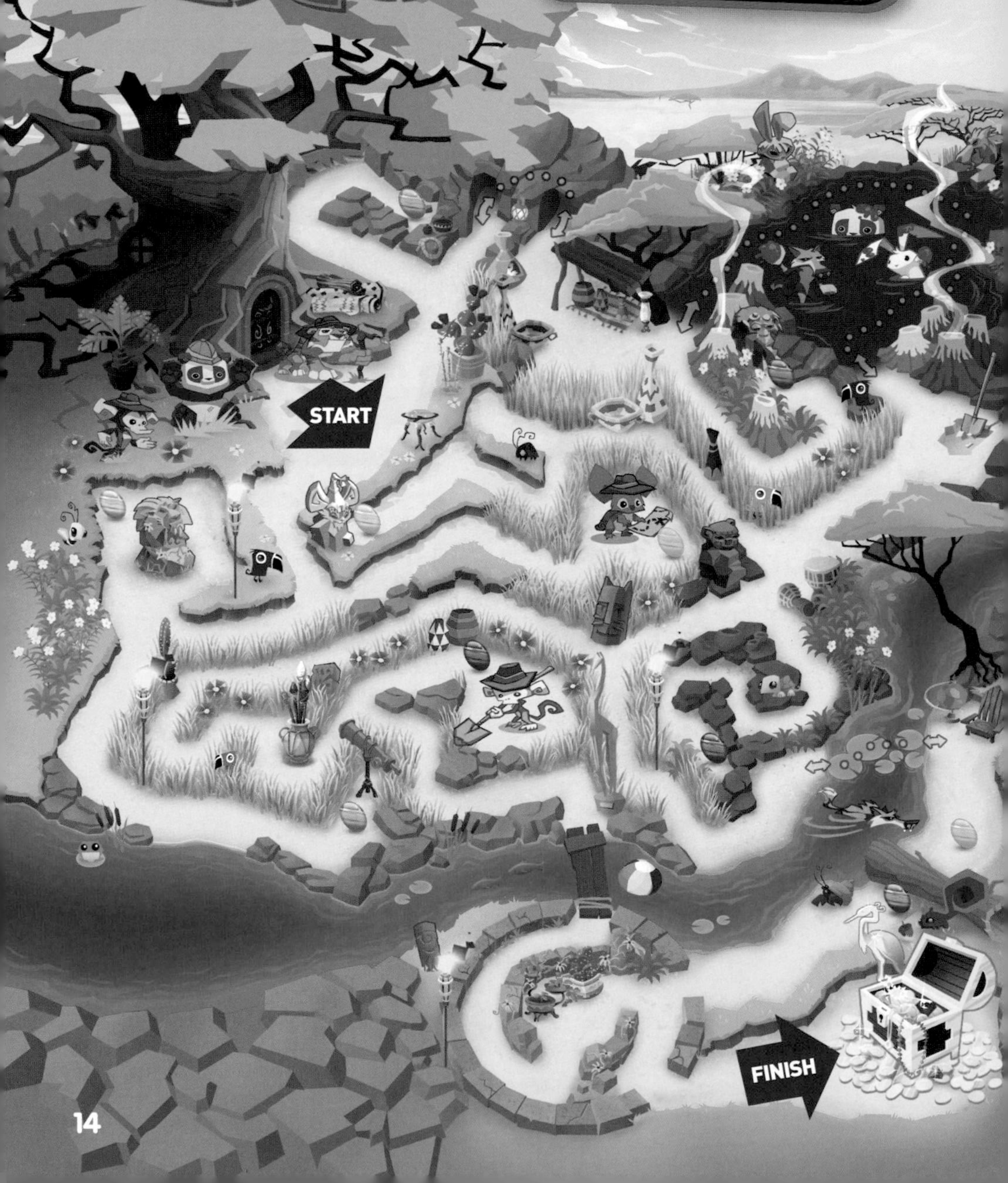

START

FINISH

Just Joking

When baby horses, or foals, are born, their legs are too long for them to bend down to eat grass!

KNOCK, KNOCK.

Who's there?
Odor.
Odor who?
I'd like to odor a large pepperoni pizza.

Monster Match

These ten monster diners have inspired the restaurant chefs. Match each of the diners to the station in the kitchen where their meal is being made.
BONUS: Find 13 forks.

Just Joking

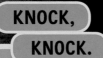

KNOCK, KNOCK.

Who's there?
Stopwatch.
Stopwatch who?
Stopwatch you're doing and open this door!

There are 21 different types of macaque monkeys that live in the world!

What in the World?

HEADS OR TAILS?

These photographs show close-up views of animal body parts. Unscramble the letters to identify each picture. Bonus: Use the highlighted letters to figure out the puzzle below.

TCA KHEWSSIR

ECLMA MUPH

SOEOM REATNL

KASEN ETUOGN

HAWEL AITL

KOEGC TOFO

CSPOTUO TNLSATCEE

LUEB-OTDEOF OYBBO OFTO

EOSTRRO MBCO

HINT: This bug would need 50 pairs of shoes.

ANSWER: _ _ _ _ _ _ _ _ _ _ _ _

19

Pick a Number ...

1 Which is the only number that is *twice* the sum of its digits?

a. 18
b. 27
c. 124
d. There is no such number.

2 Which of these metro areas is the most populated, with more than 8.9 million people?

a. Paris, France
b. Los Angeles, California, U.S.A.
c. Tokyo, Japan
d. Mexico City, Mexico

3 Which number in China is considered unlucky because its name sounds like the word for "death" in Chinese?

a. 2
b. 4
c. 67.1825
d. a zom-billion

4 True or false? From 1 to 1,000, the only written numeral with an *a* in it is the word "thousand."

5 In the expression "I'll see you in a *jiffy*," how long is a jiffy?

a. 1/100th of a second
b. 1 minute
c. 9 minutes
d. 8 hours

6 True or false? $12 + 3 - 4 + 5 + 67 + 8 + 9 = 98$

7 In which number are the letters of its written form in alphabetical order?

a. 40
b. 64
c. 76
d. 99

8 Which number is also known as *naught, zilch,* and *zip?*

a. 0
b. 9
c. 100
d. There is no such number.

9 True or false? The opposite sides of a die always add up to 7.

10 How many hexagons are on an official soccer ball?

a. 5
b. 6
c. 20
d. none

11 Assuming one second per count, how long would it take you to count to one billion?

a. 3 hours
b. 3 days
c. 32 days
d. 32 years

SIGNS
OF THE TIMES

Seeing isn't always believing. Two of these funny signs are not real. Can you figure out which two are fake?

1

2

GATOR

CROSSING

3

BEACH

4

DINOSAUR
CITY LIMIT
ELEV 5900 FT

5

7300 MUENCHEN
7400 BERN
6800 ROMA
7800 PARIS
8150 LONDON
7000 WIEN
7900 MARS
13500 NEW YORK

CAPETOWN 5100
RIO 10700
SIDNEY 10200
SINGAPORE 5400

6

DANGER
All Area Beyond This
Sign is Closed Because
Of Bear Danger

7

HA! HA! HA! HA! HA! HA! HA! HA! HA! HA! HA! HA! HA! HA! HA! HA! HA!

KNOCK, KNOCK.

Who's there?
D1.
D1 who?
D1 who knocked!

To evade predators, a puffer fish balloons up by filling its stomach with huge amounts of water.

HA! HA! HA! HA! HA! HA! HA! HA! HA! HA! HA!

Double Take

See if you can spot 12 differences in the two pictures.

A crowd of people and balloons fills a street on the Italian island of Sicily.

GO FISH!

Something's fishy at this aquarium. Find and circle the following items that are hidden in this scene.

- surfboard
- cowboy hat
- sunflower
- wrapped gift
- bike wheel
- teacup and saucer
- plate of spaghetti
- soft pretzel
- guitar

Earthly EXTREMES

1 This destination gets more than 52 feet (16 m) of snow each year, making it the snowiest place on Earth.

a. the North Pole
b. Mount Rainier, Washington, U.S.A.
c. Whistler, British Columbia, Canada
d. Antarctica

2 What is the world's longest river?

a. the Mississippi in the United States
b. the Yangtze in China
c. the Amazon in South America
d. the Nile in Africa

3 In Longyearbyen, Norway— the world's northernmost town—the sun does not rise for how long?

a. 24 hours
b. one week
c. one month
d. four months

4 **True or false?** The ocean's deepest trench is deeper than Mount Everest is high.

5 Sandboarders flock to Peru because the country has the world's tallest _____.

a. snowbanks
b. sand dunes
c. waves
d. anthills

6 The hottest known temperature on Earth was recorded in El Azizia, Libya. How hot was it?

a. 119°F (48°C)
b. 136°F (58°C)
c. 223°F (106°C)
d. 275°F (135°C)

SAHARA

7 The world's largest desert, the Sahara in Africa, is about the size of _____?

a. Rome, Italy
b. Puerto Rico
c. the Amazon rain forest
d. Australia

8 Surfers have been traveling to Nazare, Portugal, to ride some of the world's tallest waves. In 2011, surfer Garrett McNamara rode a wave that was how tall?

a. 10 feet (3 m)
b. 20 feet (6 m)
c. 50 feet (15 m)
d. 90 feet (27 m)

9 The world's deepest cave, in Ukraine, is 6,824 feet (2,080 m) from top to bottom. That's about the same as the height of _____.

a. two Eiffel Towers (Paris, France)
b. the Washington Monument (Washington, D.C., U.S.A.)
c. the Tower of Pisa (Pisa, Italy)
d. five Empire State Buildings (New York, N.Y., U.S.A.)

10 True or false? It's impossible to sink in Israel's Dead Sea.

11 The world's highest waterfall (shown at right) is _____ in Venezuela.

a. Niagara Falls
b. Iguazu Falls
c. Victoria Falls
d. Angel Falls

Just Joking

Parrot snake

KNOCK, KNOCK.
Who's there?
Who.
Who who?
Is there an owl in there?

TONGUE TWISTER!

Say this fast three times:

Crickle, cackle, crackle.

Q What did one ghost say to the other?

A Do you believe in people?

You've got to be joking ...

Q What did the jack-o'-lanterns say to their pesky little brother?

A Cut it out!

Color Coded

Some items on this Hawaiian beach have mysteriously changed color. Find 12 things that are the wrong color.

FRESH FRUIT FOR SALE

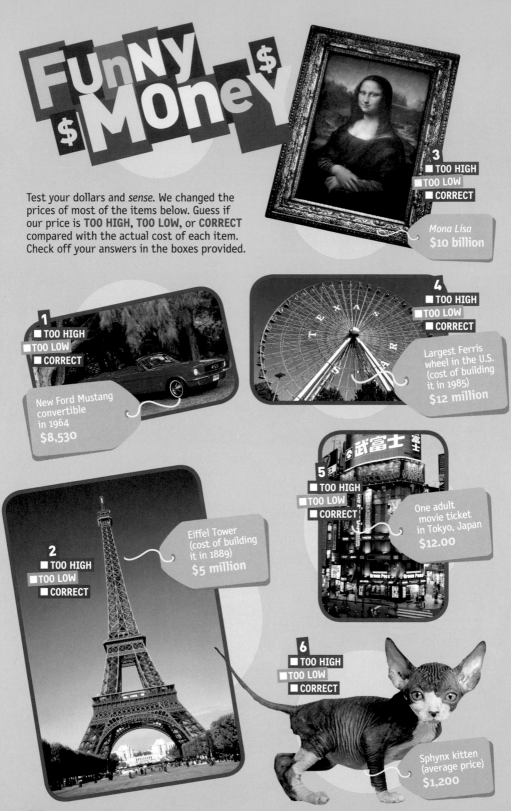

Funny $Money$

Test your dollars and *sense*. We changed the prices of most of the items below. Guess if our price is **TOO HIGH**, **TOO LOW**, or **CORRECT** compared with the actual cost of each item. Check off your answers in the boxes provided.

3
- ■ TOO HIGH
- ■ TOO LOW
- ■ CORRECT

Mona Lisa
$10 billion

1
- ■ TOO HIGH
- ■ TOO LOW
- ■ CORRECT

New Ford Mustang convertible in 1964
$8,530

4
- ■ TOO HIGH
- ■ TOO LOW
- ■ CORRECT

Largest Ferris wheel in the U.S. (cost of building it in 1985)
$12 million

5
- ■ TOO HIGH
- ■ TOO LOW
- ■ CORRECT

One adult movie ticket in Tokyo, Japan
$12.00

2
- ■ TOO HIGH
- ■ TOO LOW
- ■ CORRECT

Eiffel Tower (cost of building it in 1889)
$5 million

6
- ■ TOO HIGH
- ■ TOO LOW
- ■ CORRECT

Sphynx kitten (average price)
$1,200

SEEING SPOTS!
These photographs are close-up views of things with spots or dots. Unscramble the letters to identify each picture. Feel like you're on the spot?

SWRTITE

_____

HERAFTE

_____

COGEK

_____

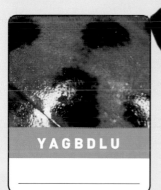

YAGBDLU

_____

MDOOIN

_____

SHFI

_____

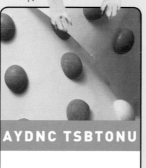

AYDNC TSBTONU

_____

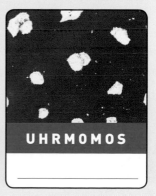

UHRMOMOS

_____

MAP MANIA!
WONDERS OF THE WORLD

1 TAJ MAHAL

Made entirely from white marble, the Taj Mahal was built by the emperor Shah Jahan for what reason?

a. to honor his deceased wife
b. to honor his children
c. to please his king
d. to create a tourist attraction in his country

2 COLOSSEUM

The Colosseum is an arena that held up to 50,000 spectators. People often came to watch fierce fighters called _____.

a. Vikings
b. barbarians
c. gladiators
d. avatars

3 CHRIST THE REDEEMER STATUE

What is the name of the mountain on which the Christ the Redeemer statue stands?

a. Mount Everest
b. Kilimanjaro
c. Corcovado
d. Mount Olympus

4 CHICHÉN ITZÁ

At certain times of year, the sunset casts shadows on this famous Mayan pyramid, creating the appearance of what kind of animal slithering down its stairs?

a. jaguar
b. lizard
c. lion
d. snake

NORTH AMERICA

MEXICO A

SOUTH AMERICA

PERU   BRAZIL

B

C

You'd have to travel the globe to visit all of the New 7 Wonders of the World, voted on in a worldwide poll. Take this quick tour to find out how much you know about these man-made marvels. Then try to match each one to the correct location on the map.

⑤ GREAT WALL

The world's longest structure ever made by humans, the Great Wall stretches about how far?

a. 100 miles (161 km)
b. 1,000 miles (1,609 km)
c. 4,500 miles (7,242 km)
d. 10,000 miles (16,093 km)

EUROPE
D.
ITALY
JORDAN
E
ASIA
A
CHINA
G
F
INDIA
AFRICA
AUSTRALIA
ANTARCTICA

⑥ MACHU PICCHU

True or false? Inca workers moved giant stones up the 7,970-foot-tall (2,429 m) mountain shown below to build Machu Picchu.

⑦ PETRA

This ancient city is carved into a cliff made of which natural material?

a. ivory
b. sandstone
c. gold
d. diamonds

8-14

THE COUNTRIES HIGHLIGHTED IN ORANGE ON THE MAP ARE EACH HOME TO ONE OF THESE WONDERS. MATCH EACH WONDER TO THE RED MARKER THAT SHOWS ITS CORRECT LOCATION.

Just Joking

African elephant

KNOCK, KNOCK.
Who's there?
Yam.
Yam who?
I yam so happy to see you!

Q What did one tornado say to the other tornado?

A See you around!

TONGUE TWISTER!

Say this fast three times:

Randy rode a raft down a rapidly rushing river.

You've **got** to be joking ...

Q What do you call a **hippo** that likes **rap music?**

A A hip-hop-o-potamus.

Bark Park

Have you ever seen a dog that resembles its owner? Look for clues in the dog park to figure out which canine belongs to which owner.

City Gone **WILD!**

Wild animals have moved into the big city, and they're fitting in a little too well. Find and circle ten wild animals hiding in this scene. Look carefully—you might see them in some funny places.

GAME ON!

These photographs show close-up views of popular games. Unscramble the letters to identify what's in each picture. **Bonus:** Use the highlighted letters to solve the puzzle below.

CSERKECH

NOOPOMLY

ESHCS

EULC

BARBECLS

YSROR!

PIRNOTAEO

NCTENCO ORFU

USMOE PTRA

HINT: What do you call icicles hanging from a snowman's face?

ANSWER: __ __ O __ __ __ __ __ __ __ D

Just Joking

Cooks cook

cupcakes quickly.

DYNAMIC DUOS

These photographs show close-up views of pairs. Unscramble the letters to identify what's in each picture. **Bonus:** Use the highlighted letters to solve the puzzle below.

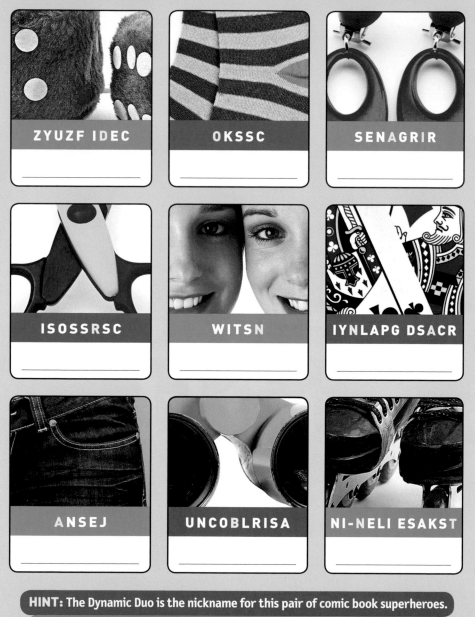

ZYUZF IDEC

OKSSC

SENAGRIR

ISOSSRSC

WITSN

IYNLAPG DSACR

ANSEJ

UNCOBLRISA

NI-NELI ESAKST

HINT: The Dynamic Duo is the nickname for this pair of comic book superheroes.

ANSWER: __ __ __ __ __ **M** __ __ __ __ __ __ __ __ **B** __ __ __ __

ALSO KNOWN AS

Chinese New Year—also known as Lunar New Year—celebrates the first day of the Chinese calendar. Figure out the three-word phrase that describes each of the numbered scenes at this Chinese New Year's parade. The first and last words always begin with **a**, and the middle word always begins with **k**. For example, the answer to number 1 is "ape knits alphabet." Lost in the crowd?

Double Take

See if you can spot 12 differences in the two pictures.

Visitors enjoy Chinese New Year decorations at Yu Garden in Shanghai, China.

Guernsey cow

Just Joking

KNOCK, KNOCK.

Who's there?
Olive.
Olive who?
Olive you.

Q

Why do birds **fly south** in the **winter?**

A It's easier than walking.

EMILY: Did you know you were built upside down?
ADAM: What do you mean?
EMILY: Your nose runs and your feet smell.

HA HA HA!

WAIT! I'M NOT NUTS! I'M JUST NUTS FOR YOU!

Toy Stories

1 Which putty-like material was invented in the 1950s to clean wallpaper but today is used by kids in arts-and-crafts projects?
- **a.** paste
- **b.** pancake batter
- **c.** Play-Doh
- **d.** WALL-E

2 TRUE OR FALSE? HEXBUGS ARE MICRO, ROBOTIC, INSECTLIKE TOYS THAT REACT TO THEIR ENVIRONMENT.

HEXBUG

BARBIE DOLL

3 Barbie fashion dolls have portrayed all the following careers except _____.
- **a.** fighter pilot
- **b.** architect
- **c.** farmer
- **d.** president

SLINKY

4 What did a Slinky toy do when scientists aboard the space shuttle *Discovery* played with it?
- **a.** It unwound.
- **b.** It did not float.
- **c.** It walked *up* stairs.
- **d.** It did not slink at all.

FURBY

5 Which company created the Xbox?
- **a.** Apple
- **b.** Boxes-R-Us
- **c.** Microsoft
- **d.** Xerox

6 An online dictionary and app can help you communicate with an interactive Furby toy. What language does Furby speak?
- **a.** Furbese
- **b.** Furbalian
- **c.** Fur Latin
- **d.** Furbish

7 Which of the following is not a name of a Monster High fashion doll?
- **a.** Ghoulia Yelps
- **b.** Cruela D'Zilla
- **c.** Clawdeen Wolf
- **d.** Draculaura

8 How many kids can fit comfortably in the largest Radio Flyer wagon ever built?
- **a.** 7
- **b.** 15
- **c.** 1,000
- **d.** 75

 9 Which of the following is not the name of a Fijit Friends toy?
- **a.** Logan
- **b.** Serafina
- **c.** Thyme
- **d.** Sage

10 **True or False?** Silly Putty was used to help American astronauts during their missions to the moon.

11 **True or False?** Matchbox cars were given their name because they were originally made from old matchboxes.

MATCHBOX CARS

 12 The world record for tossing this toy is 693 feet (211 m). Which is the name of this flying toy?
- **a.** Cabbage Patch Kid
- **b.** Frisbee
- **c.** Hula-Hoop
- **d.** Wiffle ball

What in the World?

FUN IN THE SUN

These photographs show close-up and faraway views of things at the beach. Unscramble the letters to identify each picture. Bonus: Use the highlighted letters to solve the puzzle below.

VEWA

_____

MSIW RNSUKT

_____

HRIAC

_____

SHLASESLE

_____

ABRC

_____

LSUEAGL

_____

BILSOTAA

_____

ASGSLUESNS

_____

ILFP-POFL

_____

HINT: You'll need all of your toes and awesome surfing skills to do this.

ANSWER: ___ ___ ___ ___ ___ ___ ___ ___

46

Make a SPLASH!

Many expressions don't mean what they say. For example, if you have butterflies in your stomach, that really means you're nervous. This swimming pool scene shows ten expressions exactly as they are worded. For example, number one is **"pie in the sky."** Can you figure out which expression appears in each of the numbered pictures?

LOCKER ROOMS

SIGNS
OF THE TIMES

Seeing isn't always believing. Two of these funny signs are not real. Can you figure out which two are fake?

1

2 WHICH WAY

3 TEAKETTLE JUNCTION
RACETRACK 6
HUNTER MTN 18

NO HUNTING

4 NEXT 96 km

5 ALIEN PARKING

6 WATCH FOR ICE

7

Mythical Mix-Up

WELCOME, CREATURES!

NESSIE

MEDUSA

TROLL

GENIE

TROLL

CYCLOPS

GIANT

UNICORN

YETI

BIGFOOT

FAUN

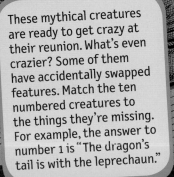

These mythical creatures are ready to get crazy at their reunion. What's even crazier? Some of them have accidentally swapped features. Match the ten numbered creatures to the things they're missing. For example, the answer to number 1 is "The dragon's tail is with the leprechaun."

Just Joking

KNOCK, KNOCK.

Who's there?
Ivana.
Ivana who?
Ivana you to
let me in.

Seals mostly eat fish, squid, mollusks, and crustaceans.

WILD RANGE

These photographs show close-up views of animals that live in Southeast Asia, a region covering 11 countries including Malaysia, Indonesia, and Vietnam. Unscramble the letters to identify what's in each picture. Bonus: Use the highlighted letters to solve the puzzle below.

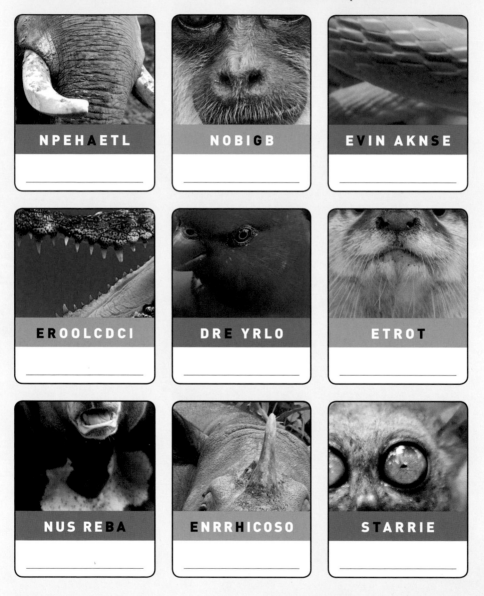

NPEHAETL

_____

NOBIGB

_____

EVIN AKNSE

_____

EROOLCDCI

_____

DRE YRLO

_____

ETROT

_____

NUS REBA

_____

ENRRHICOSO

_____

STARRIE

_____

HINT: Why are frogs so happy?

ANSWER: T _ _ _ Y E _ _ _
W H _ T _ _ _ E _ _ _ U _ _ _ _ H _ M.

Find the HIDDEN ANIMALS

Animals often blend in with their environments for protection. Find each animal listed below in one of the pictures. Write the letter of the correct picture next to each animal's name.

1. sea star   _____
2. crab   _____
3. arctic hare   _____
4. owl   _____
5. gazelle   _____
6. chameleon   _____

Bugging Out

1 Houseflies can taste with their _____.

a. feet
b. ears
c. tongue
c. wings

2 **True or false?** Honeybees kill more people each year than snakes.

TERMITE QUEEN

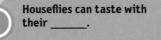

3 How many eggs can a termite queen lay every day?

a. 10
b. 300
c. 5,000
d. 30,000

4 Where might you find the ears of certain types of crickets and grasshoppers?

a. under the tail
b. on the head
c. on the front legs
d. at the ends of the antennae

5 **True or false?** Mosquito-borne diseases have caused more human deaths than all the wars in history.

GOLIATH BEETLE

6 What is the smallest insect on Earth?

a. a stink bug
b. a fairyfly
c. a no-see-um
d. a fire ant

7 Goliath beetles found in Africa are Earth's heaviest insects. How much do they weigh?

a. 2 ounces (57 grams)
b. 4 ounces (113 grams)
c. 8 ounces (226 grams)
d. 1 pound (.5 kg)

8 What is the name of Earth's biggest spider, which is 11 inches (28 cm) wide with one-inch (2.5 cm) fangs and eight eyes?

a. dino spider
b. Goliath birdeater tarantula
c. Guatemalan huntsman spider
d. camel spider

9 How many insect species do scientists know of so far?

a. 300,000
b. 500,000
c. 1 million
d. 1.5 million

FLIK, FROM
A BUG'S LIFE

10 What is the only insect on Earth with only one ear?

a. elephant beetle
b. praying mantis
c. stick bug
d. ant

11 **True or false?** One little brown bat can eat 10,000 to 20,000 insects in one night.

12 Pound for pound (kg for kg), which is the world's strongest animal?

a. dragonfly
b. Goliath birdeater tarantula
c. flea
d. rhinoceros beetle

13 A famous fossil found in Bolivia in 1979 preserves a dragonfly that lived 250 million years ago and was the biggest insect ever known. How wide was its wingspan?

a. as wide as your hand
b. as wide as your foot is long
c. as wide as a ruler is long
d. as wide as a skateboard is long

FOSSILIZED
DRAGONFLY

Obstacle Course Chaos

This gym class obstacle course has everyone tangled up. Using the series of clues, can you figure out which student accidentally caused the chaos?

The person who caused the chaos ...

- is wearing mismatched socks.
- has an untied shoelace.
- is wearing glasses.
- is wearing a shirt backward.
- has brown hair.
- is not wearing a hat.

Panda-monium!

Pandas may look like they stand out in a crowd, but believe it or not, in their snowy and rocky environment they're totally camouflaged. Take a look at the black-and-white objects below and see if you can find all the items on the list.

- 6 soccer balls
- 4 pushpins
- 7 chess pieces
- 6 plastic utensils
- 5 clothespins
- 4 things you look through
- 3 number 8s
- 3 club cars
- 3 pandas
- 5 other animals

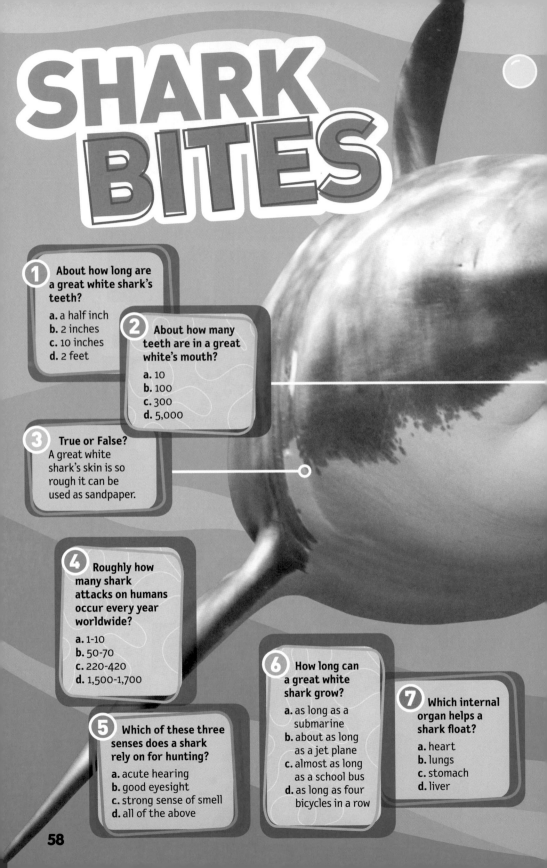

SHARK BITES

1 About how long are a great white shark's teeth?
- **a.** a half inch
- **b.** 2 inches
- **c.** 10 inches
- **d.** 2 feet

2 About how many teeth are in a great white's mouth?
- **a.** 10
- **b.** 100
- **c.** 300
- **d.** 5,000

3 True or False? A great white shark's skin is so rough it can be used as sandpaper.

4 Roughly how many shark attacks on humans occur every year worldwide?
- **a.** 1-10
- **b.** 50-70
- **c.** 220-420
- **d.** 1,500-1,700

5 Which of these three senses does a shark rely on for hunting?
- **a.** acute hearing
- **b.** good eyesight
- **c.** strong sense of smell
- **d.** all of the above

6 How long can a great white shark grow?
- **a.** as long as a submarine
- **b.** about as long as a jet plane
- **c.** almost as long as a school bus
- **d.** as long as four bicycles in a row

7 Which internal organ helps a shark float?
- **a.** heart
- **b.** lungs
- **c.** stomach
- **d.** liver

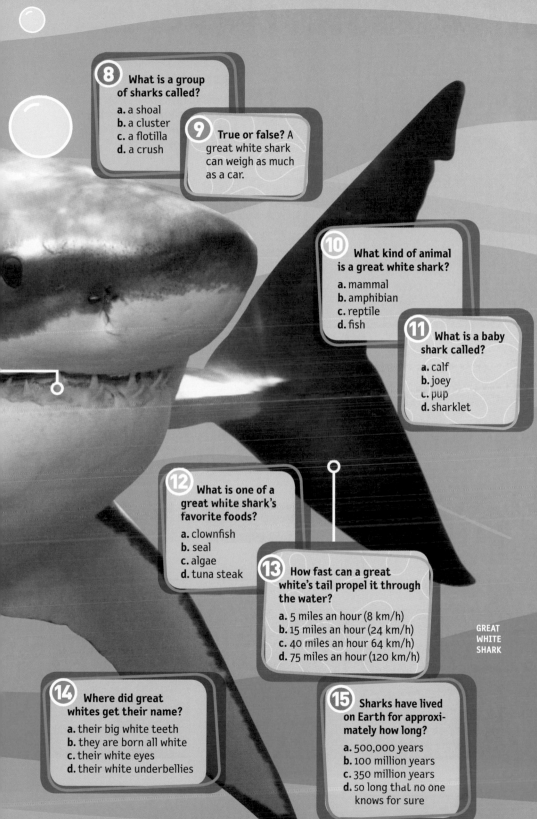

8 What is a group of sharks called?
- **a.** a shoal
- **b.** a cluster
- **c.** a flotilla
- **d.** a crush

9 True or false? A great white shark can weigh as much as a car.

10 What kind of animal is a great white shark?
- **a.** mammal
- **b.** amphibian
- **c.** reptile
- **d.** fish

11 What is a baby shark called?
- **a.** calf
- **b.** joey
- **c.** pup
- **d.** sharklet

12 What is one of a great white shark's favorite foods?
- **a.** clownfish
- **b.** seal
- **c.** algae
- **d.** tuna steak

13 How fast can a great white's tail propel it through the water?
- **a.** 5 miles an hour (8 km/h)
- **b.** 15 miles an hour (24 km/h)
- **c.** 40 miles an hour 64 km/h)
- **d.** 75 miles an hour (120 km/h)

GREAT WHITE SHARK

14 Where did great whites get their name?
- **a.** their big white teeth
- **b.** they are born all white
- **c.** their white eyes
- **d.** their white underbellies

15 Sharks have lived on Earth for approximately how long?
- **a.** 500,000 years
- **b.** 100 million years
- **c.** 350 million years
- **d.** so long that no one knows for sure

HELLO, YELLOW
These images show views of things that are yellow. Unscramble the letters to identify what's in each picture.

OESSR
_____

LSDIGNKCU
_____

AAANBN
_____

UAMRDST
_____

ORGF
_____

NSAISRI
_____

PHGNOISP ASTCR
_____

ANRI SBTOO
_____

RUFBTLSITEE
_____

Just Joking

LITTLE GHOUL:
No fair! Why can you go to the Halloween party when I can't?

BIG GHOUL:
Because I'm the mummy, that's why!

Q
What do you call a thief who falls in wet cement?

A
A hardened criminal.

What do you do when a pony gets sick?

Send him to the horse-pital.

61

The Wide WORLD OF SPORTS

① One of the world's most popular sports is known as "soccer" in Australia, Canada, New Zealand, and the U.S. But what is it called in most other countries?

a. kickball
b. goalkeeper
c. World Cup
d. football

② True or false? Each of the five Olympic rings is a different color to represent the five major regions of the world involved in the Olympics.

③ What is the name of the sport, popular in both Canada and Scotland, that involves a broom?

a. ice hockey
b. lacrosse
c. sweeping
d. curling

④ True or false? In Afghanistan, the sport of kite fighting involves cutting your opponents' kite strings so that your kite can fly the highest and longest.

⑤ The tropical island nation of Jamaica surprised the world when it took part in what sport in the 1988 Winter Olympics?

a. swimming
b. running
c. bobsledding
d. water polo

⑥ The world's heaviest sumo wrestler weighed 630 pounds (287 kg). That's almost as heavy as a male _____.

a.
brown bear

b.
sheep

c.
blue whale

d.
golden retriever

7 There are ten different sports in a decathlon. Which of the following is not a decathlon sport?
a. long jump
b. pole vault
c. marathon
d. javelin throw

8 Which American football team won the first ever Super Bowl, played in 1967?
a. Green Bay Packers
b. Dallas Cowboys
c. New Orleans Saints
d. Kansas City Chiefs

9 This skateboarder, nick-named "The Birdman," was the first ever to land a trick called the 900—that's two and a half turns in the air!
a. Shaun White
b. Andy Macdonald
c. Tony Hawk
d. Ryan Sheckler

10 Which country has won the most Olympic medals?
a. Italy
b. United States
c. Germany
d. Greece

11 What is the name of the instrument that fans could be heard blowing during the 2010 FIFA World Cup?
a. harmonica
b. bullhorn
c. trumpet
d. vuvuzela

12 True or false? In Malaysia, some athletes play tennis using their legs and feet instead of racquets.

BEST OF THE NORTHWEST

These photos show close-up views of things in the Pacific Northwest, U.S.A. Unscramble the letters to identify each picture. **Bonus:** Use the highlighted letters to figure out the puzzle below.

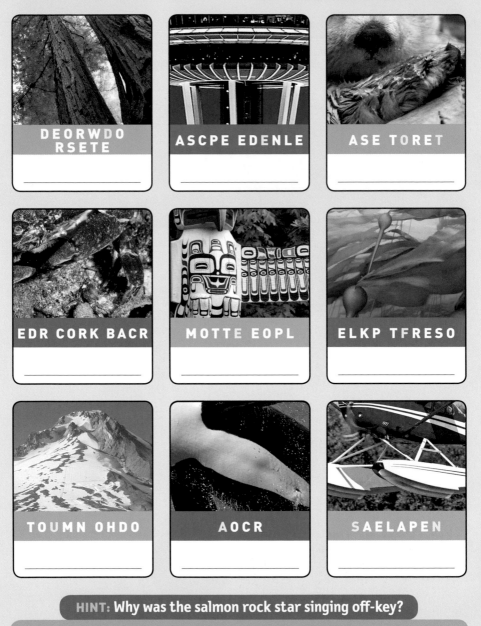

DEORWDO RSETE

_____

ASCPE EDENLE

_____

ASE TORET

_____

EDR CORK BACR

_____

MOTTE EOPL

_____

ELKP TFRESO

_____

TOUMN OHDO

_____

AOCR

_____

SAELAPEN

_____

HINT: Why was the salmon rock star singing off-key?

ANSWER: _H_ __ _E_ __ _E D_ __ _T_ _N_ __ __ _I_ _H_

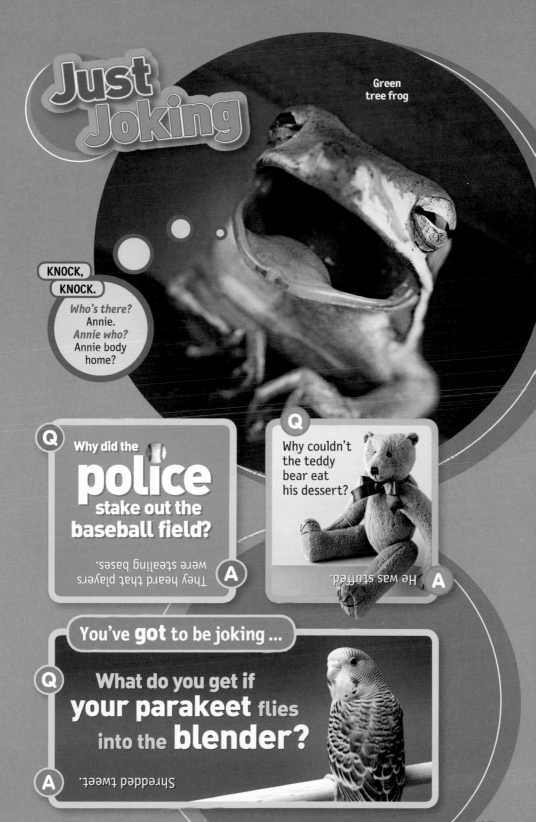

Just Joking

Green tree frog

KNOCK, KNOCK.

Who's there?
Annie.
Annie who?
Annie body home?

Q Why did the **police** stake out the baseball field?

A They heard that players were stealing bases.

Q Why couldn't the teddy bear eat his dessert?

A He was stuffed.

You've **got** to be joking ...

Q What do you get if **your parakeet** flies into the **blender?**

A Shredded tweet.

Famous PAIRS

ROBIN AND BATMAN

1 At whose home do Woody and Buzz end up at the end of the movie *Toy Story 3*?
- **a.** Andy's
- **b.** Sid's
- **c.** Bonnie's
- **d.** Lotso's

2 When not wearing their crime-fighting capes, Batman and Robin are known as _____ and _____.
- **a.** Peter Parker and Dexter Bennett
- **b.** Bruce Banner and Jim Wilson
- **c.** Bruce Wayne and Dick Grayson
- **d.** Clark Kent and Jimmy Olsen

3 Who travels with and protects his fellow Hobbit, Frodo Baggins, during many adventures in The Lord of the Rings movies?
- **a.** Bilbo Baggins
- **b.** Grima Wormtongue
- **c.** Dandumb Smith
- **d.** Samwise Gamgee

FRODO

4 Which TV best friends dined on spaghetti tacos?
- **a.** Bert and Ernie
- **b.** Carly and Sam
- **c.** Flick and Flack
- **d.** Drake and Josh

5 **True or False?** *Animaniacs* television show characters Pinky and the Brain are mice.

6 Which pop culture legends fell in love on the set of their first television commercial for Mattel Toys in 1961?
- **a.** Fred and Wilma Flintstone
- **b.** Mr. and Mrs. Potato Head
- **c.** Barbie and Ken
- **d.** Daffy Duck and Daisy Duck

WILMA AND FRED FLINTSTONE

7 What are the names of the two friends who use science to prove or disprove popular myths on the TV show *MythBusters?*

a. Simon and Randy
b. Calvin and Hobbes
c. Thelma and Daphne
d. Jamie and Adam

8 **True or False?** Mario and Luigi from the Mario Bros. video games are two New York City cousins who are musicians.

9 In the Legend of Zelda games, Link must often rescue Princess Zelda in which fictional setting?

a. Hyrule
b. Narnia
c. Oz
d. No-rules

10 Who is one of Brick Heck's best friends on the TV show *The Middle*?

a. Brad
b. Carly
c. his backpack
d. his no. 2 pencil

MARIO AND LUIGI

11 In which decade did Mickey and Minnie Mouse share their first kiss?

a. the 1920s
b. the 1950s
c. the 1960s
d. the 1980s

12 Which school of study do movie monster friends Mike and Sulley attend at Monsters University?

a. School of Scaring
b. School of Liberal Arts & Monstrosities
c. School of Business
d. School of Engineering

MIKE AND SULLEY
FROM *MONSTERS, INC.*

Up, Up, and Away

Can you find the sky path that leads to the lost kite? Some paths may take you through grass, kites, clouds, and trees.

Just Joking

Camels have long eyelashes that protect their eyes from sand and dust.

KNOCK, KNOCK.

Who's there?
Bacon.
Bacon who?
Whatcha bacon?
It smells great!

TRIVIA TECH ZONE

1 For its 1982 "Person of the Year," U.S. magazine *Time* put _____ on its cover.

a. a bald eagle   c. a computer
b. the space shuttle   d. a race car

2 Which country leads the world in Internet usage with more than **500 million** users?

a. Japan   c. United States
b. South Africa   d. China

3 Apple announced that as of February 2013, more than _____ songs had been downloaded from its music store, iTunes.

a. 1 million   c. 25 billion
b. 55 million   d. 1 trillion

4 About how many **computers existed** in the world in 1953?

a. 0   c. 100
b. 1   d. 1 million

5 In 2012, Facebook reached _____ billion users!

a. 1   c. 100
b. 10   d. 890

6 "Tweets," brief messages sent via Twitter, must be how many characters or fewer?

a. 140   c. 210
b. 188   d. 570

7 True or false? As of 2012, YouTube received about 4 billion views per day.

8 Melissa Thompson of England set a world record for text-messaging speed by typing a **26-word** sentence in _____.

a. 1.3 seconds   c. 1 minute, 5 seconds
b. 25.94 seconds   d. 3.7 minutes

9 AlphaDog is a **robot designed** to go into battle with military troops. It can trek over rough terrain for 20 miles (32.2 km) while carrying ____ of gear.

a. 40 pounds (18 kg) c. 250 pounds (113 kg)
b. 140 pounds (64 kg) d. 400 pounds (181 kg)

10 True or false? In 2006, an Australian citizen tried to sell the nation of New Zealand through eBay, with a starting bid of 1 cent.

11 In 1981, twelve engineers at IBM secretly developed the first personal computer (PC). What was their code name?

a. Dirty Dozen c. Magnificent Minds
b. 12 Brains d. Dozen Darlings

12 Four game players in Austria hold the world's record for longest video game marathon using a **mobile phone.** How long did the game last?

a. 3 hours 15 minutes
b. 6 hours
c. 12 hours 8 minutes
d. 24 hours 10 minutes

A CIRCUIT BOARD
DIRECTING ELECTRICAL
CURRENT WITHIN A
COMPUTER

Just Joking

KNOCK, KNOCK.

Who's there?
Sand.
Sand who?
Sand me a text when you are ready to leave.

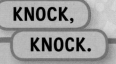

The lionhead goldfish gets its name from a growth on its head called a wen. It covers its head, cheeks, and gills.

SPELLBOUND

This wacky wizard is trying to make ten different animals magically appear. But he keeps creating objects that rhyme with the animals' names instead. For example, number one is a balloon rather than a baboon. Can you figure out which animals he meant to create? Bonus: Do other animal names rhyme with any of these objects?

Just Joking

Northern elephant seal

KNOCK, KNOCK.
Who's there?
Ima.
Ima who?
Ima little short and can't reach the doorbell.

Funny List

Four ways to tell you're at Earth's birthday party:

1. There's mud pie instead of cake.
2. The decorations are all natural.
3. The party favors are out of this world.
4. Earth makes a wish on a shooting star instead of blowing out candles.

TONGUE TWISTER!

Say this fast three times:

Corn on the cob makes Bob the slob's slobber stop.

You've **got** to be joking...

Q Why did the **koala get hired** for the job?

A He had all the right koala-fications.

These photographs show close-up views of animals that live in the rain forest. Unscramble the letters to identify what's in each picture.
Bonus: Use the highlighted letters to solve the puzzle below.

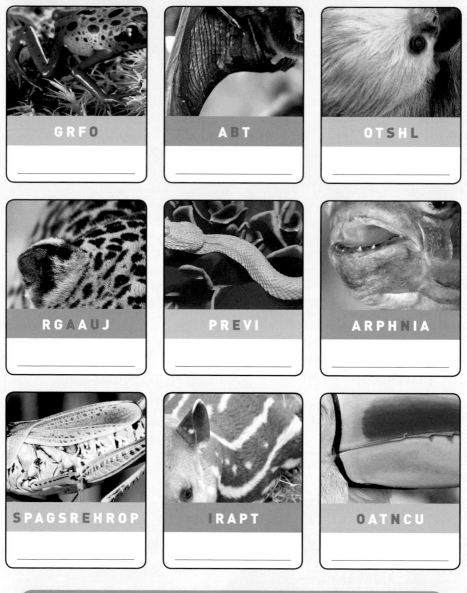

GRFO

ABT

OTSHL

RGAAUJ

PREVI

ARPHNIA

SPAGSREHROP

IRAPT

OATNCU

HINT: Where would you go to buy bananas from a loud primate?

ANSWER: _ H W _ _ R M _ K _ Y _ S _ E _

76

Just Joking

HA! HA! HA! HA! HA! HA! HA!

Q What do you feed a noisy dog?

A Hush puppies.

Porcupines can grow new quills to replace the ones that fall out.

What did the **porcupine** say to the **cactus?**

"Is that you, Mommy?"

Q What did the banana do when the monkey chased it?

A The banana split.

Q Why did the watchmaker enjoy his vacation?

A Because he learned to unwind.

THE AMAZING HUMAN MACHINE

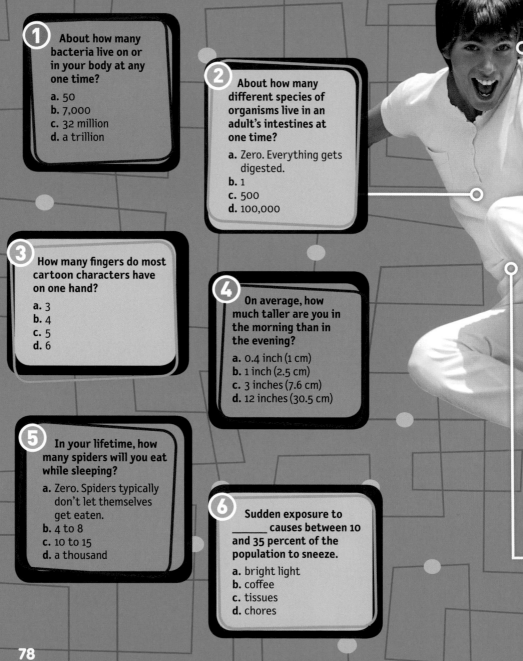

1 About how many bacteria live on or in your body at any one time?

a. 50
b. 7,000
c. 32 million
d. a trillion

2 About how many different species of organisms live in an adult's intestines at one time?

a. Zero. Everything gets digested.
b. 1
c. 500
d. 100,000

3 How many fingers do most cartoon characters have on one hand?

a. 3
b. 4
c. 5
d. 6

4 On average, how much taller are you in the morning than in the evening?

a. 0.4 inch (1 cm)
b. 1 inch (2.5 cm)
c. 3 inches (7.6 cm)
d. 12 inches (30.5 cm)

5 In your lifetime, how many spiders will you eat while sleeping?

a. Zero. Spiders typically don't let themselves get eaten.
b. 4 to 8
c. 10 to 15
d. a thousand

6 Sudden exposure to _____ causes between 10 and 35 percent of the population to sneeze.

a. bright light
b. coffee
c. tissues
d. chores

7 What is the largest number of children born to one woman in a lifetime?

a. 4
b. 18
c. 69
d. 101

8 How many times a day does the average person pass gas?

a. 1
b. 14
c. 134
d. No one knows because no one will tell.

9 **True or false?** The only place where organisms cannot live on your body is in your eyelashes.

10 The human heart can create enough pressure to squirt blood this far.

a. 14 inches (36 cm)
b. 2 feet (61 cm)
c. 30 feet (9 m)
d. 1 mile (1.6 km)

11 How often do people shed their entire layer of outer skin cells?

a. every 2 to 4 weeks
b. every 6 months
c. once a year
d. every time they watch a scary movie

12 The average human body contains enough carbon to make how many pencils?

a. 1
b. 150
c. 900
d. 10,000

Trading
Places

These animals got mixed up! They are all in the wrong habitats. Write each animal's name (listed below) in the space beside its correct habitat name.

- orangutan
- camel
- brown bear
- bullfrog
- clown fish
- giraffe
- emperor penguin

1 Pond
North America

2 Savanna
Africa

3 Desert
Africa

5 Ocean
Antarctica

6 Rain
Forest
Asia

4 Coral
Reef
Australia

7 Tundra
North
America

Mystery Maize

Help these kids find their way through this creepy cornfield without getting blocked by spooky things in their path.

START

FINISH

Funniest Fads
OF ALL TIME

1 Where did the idea for Hula-Hoops, which became a craze in the late 1950s, come from?

a. bamboo hoops used by Australian kids
b. tire rims used by Swedish kids
c. metal hoops used by construction workers
d. circular branches used by monkeys

2 **True or false?** Swallowing as many gold-fish as possible was once a popular fad among college students.

3 Stuffing as many people as possible into a _____ became popular in the 1950s.

a. mail truck
b. closet
c. phone booth
d. movie theater

4 In 1924, Alvin "Shipwreck" Kelly started a fad called pole-sitting when he climbed to the top of a flagpole—and sat on it. How long did he sit?

a. 30 minutes
b. 3 hours 22 minutes
c. 9 hours
d. 13 hours 13 minutes

5 **True or false?** The art of tie-dyeing had been around for thousands of years before tie-dyed T-shirts became popular in the 1960s and 1970s.

6 In the 1960s, women piled their hair on top of their heads and teased it until it was the shape of a _____, for which this hairstyle was named.

a. poodle
b. beehive
c. nest
d. mullet

7 While listening to friends complain about their unruly pets, Gary Dahl got an idea for a "pet" that would always be obedient and would never need to be walked. What was this pet, which became a top seller in late 1975?

a. a pet rock
b. a cat-dog
c. a stuffed toy animal
d. a pet stick

8 Mood rings, popular in the 1970s, were filled with liquid crystal that changed color with the wearer's body temperature, supposedly reflecting the mood of the ring wearer. Match the ring color to the correct mood.

- **a.** dark blue
- **b.** green
- **c.** amber
- **d.** black
- **e.** average
- **f.** stressed
- **g.** a little nervous
- **h.** happy

9 Which dance style took over nightclubs in the 1970s?

- **a.** breakdancing
- **b.** disco
- **c.** moshing
- **d.** the Twist

10 During which decade did the Rubik's Cube originally become popular?

- **a.** the 1930s
- **b.** the 1950s
- **c.** the 1980s
- **d.** the 2000s

11 During the 1990s, kids collected small stuffed animals called what?

- **a.** Jumping Jacks
- **b.** Beanie Babies
- **c.** Stuffies
- **d.** Hacky Sacks

RUBIK'S CUBE

12 In 2009, these colorful rubber bracelets, in shapes such as animals and letters, appeared on wrists everywhere.

- **a.** Silly Bandz
- **b.** charm bracelets
- **c.** tennis bracelets
- **d.** friendship bracelets

13 In the 2000s, hundreds of people—communicating by mobile phone—started showing up in public places to do funny things, such as dance or have a pillow fight. What is this fad called?

- **a.** flash mob
- **b.** crowd craze
- **c.** flocking
- **d.** block party

SPOTTED IN NATURE

These photographs show close-up views of things with spots. Unscramble the letters to identify each picture. Bonus: Use the highlighted letters to solve the puzzle below.

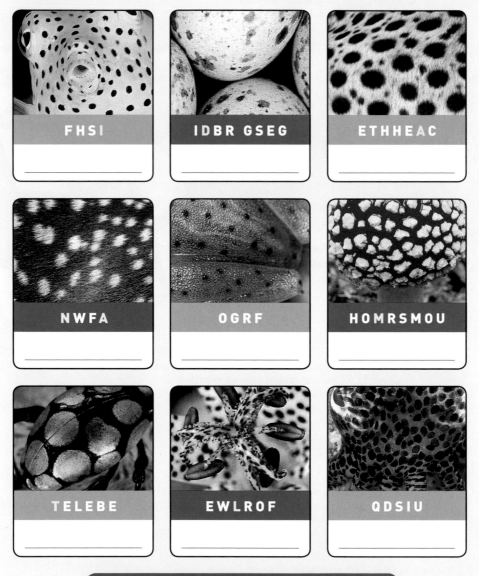

FHSI

_____

IDBR GSEG

_____

ETHHEAC

_____

NWFA

_____

OGRF

_____

HOMRSMOU

_____

TELEBE

_____

EWLROF

_____

QDSIU

_____

HINT: Call them spots or dots, this canine has lots.

ANSWER: __ __ __ __ __ __ __ __ A __ __

Just Joking

Tree squirrels are sometimes called "living fossils" because they look basically the same as they did five million years ago.

KNOCK,

KNOCK.

Who's there?
Tom Sawyer.
Tom Sawyer who?
Tom sawyer underpants.

PIRATES' COVE

1 **True or false?**
Pirates attacked other ships to sink them.

2 **True or false?** Only men were pirates.

3 **What did infamous pirate Blackbeard put in his beard to scare sailors on the ships he captured?**

a. black dye   c. daggers
b. burning ropes   d. rats

4 **In the 17th century, pirates in the Caribbean were also known as what?**

a. buccaneers
b. musketeers
c. avatars
d. cosmonauts

5 **True or false?** Most pirates **buried** their **treasure.**

6 **If an 18th-century pirate demanded "belly timber," what would he be asking for?**

a. wood   c. food
b. gold   d. a new ship

7 **What was a "Jolly Roger" in pirate lingo?**

a. a happy pirate whose real name was Roger James
b. a pirate ship
c. a candy eaten by pirates
d. a flag flown on a pirate ship

8 **A pirate who lost a leg during a sea battle or sailing accident wore an artificial wooden limb called ___.**

a. a peg leg   c. a crutch
b. a spindle   d. a tree limb

9 True or false? The character Jack Sparrow from the *Pirates of the Caribbean* movies was based on a real pirate.

10 *Queen Anne's Revenge* was the flagship of which pirate?

a. Black Bart
b. Sam Bellamy
c. Blackbeard
d. Henry Morgan

11 If a pirate ordered his crew to "feed the fish," he wanted them to:

a. throw someone overboard
b. keep an eye on his treasure
c. make dinner
d. feed his pet fish

12 Which of the following were standard pirate punishments?

a. flogging (whipping)
b. marooning (leaving someone on an island alone)
c. keelhauling (pulling someone under the bottom of a ship with a rope)
d. all of the above

13 True or false? Most pirates wore earrings as a fashion statement.

14 An 18th-century pirate would have used which of the following weapons?

a. sword
b. cannon
c. whip
d. all of the above

15 True or false? Some pirates kept parrots on board their ships.

Iguana

Just Joking

KNOCK,
KNOCK.

Who's there?
Turnip.
Turnip who?
Turnip the heat.
It's freezing in here!

TONGUE TWISTER!

Say this fast three times:

Six thick socks on seven thin sirs.

Q Who **chews** on trees and **sings?**

A Justin Beaver.

Q

What did the polar bear order for lunch?

An iceberg-er.

A

Mousetrap

A tiny mouse has sneaked into this restaurant and caused chaos. Find 20 things in the dining room that the mouse has nibbled on, and then find the mouse. We've circled one nibble for you.

Take the Plunge

Help this scuba diver clean up the coral reef. Find the following items that don't belong under the sea:

- toy car
- in-line skate
- wristwatch
- peanut butter
- beach ball
- sneaker
- sunglasses
- bananas
- suntan lotion
- scooter
- boat oar

What in the World?

INTO DARKNESS
These photographs show close-up views of things found underground. Unscramble the letters to identify what's in each picture.
Bonus: Use the black letters to solve the puzzle below.

TANS

_____

OTOSR

_____

ILMDEEIPL

_____

LEOM

_____

ETEBLE

_____

AAARLTNUT

_____

VARAL

_____

SLIFSO

_____

ADCCIA

_____

HINT: When Frankenstein's monster sits on potatoes, you get this.

ANSWER: _ O N _ _ _ _ _ A _ H _ _ _ _ _ _ T O E S

93

MARK YOUR CALENDAR

1 The mysterious structure of **Stonehenge** is thought to be as old as the _____.

a. sun
b. Grand Canyon
c. Egyptian pyramids
d. Leaning Tower of Pisa

2 What type of competition takes place at the **annual Wimbledon Championships?**

a. tennis
b. skydiving
c. swimming
d. extreme biking

3 In which celebration is it traditional for people to dance through the streets wearing a **dragon costume?**

a. Midnight Festival
b. Mardi Gras
c. Presidents' Day
d. Chinese New Year

4 During the Holi holiday in India, people celebrate by throwing what at each other?

a. colored water, paint, and powder
b. pies
c. paper money
d. fruit

5 True or false? Wrapping a pole with colorful ribbons is an important part of May Day celebrations.

6 If you have **triskaidekaphobia, you have a fear of** _____.

a. math
b. the number 13
c. tricycles
d. the number 3

STONEHENGE

7 What is a **leap year?**

a. a year honoring the game of leapfrog

b. a year in which an extra day is added to February

c. a year in which a day is subtracted from April

d. a year celebrating the kangaroo in Australia

8 True or false? A day on Earth is longer than a day on Mars.

10 True or false? On April 1 in France, people play pranks by sticking a paper fish to the backs of their unsuspecting victims.

9 What is it called when a **second full moon appears** in one calendar month?

a. Daylight Savings Time

b. an extra moon month

c. a blue moon

d. a lunar month

11 If it is summer and you can still see the **sun at midnight,** you may be _____.

a. in Puerto Rico

b. in Norway

c. near the equator

d. in a time warp

12 Where could you attend the Monkey Buffet Festival in which monkeys are presented with a table filled with fruits and vegetables?

a. Thailand

b. New Zealand

c. California

d. Chile

13 Thousands of people attend a **festival in Spain** in order to hurl what at each other?

a. mud

b. raw eggs

c. tomatoes

d. snowballs

Find the HIDDEN ANIMALS

Animals often blend in with their environments for protection. Find the animals listed below in the photographs. Write the letter of the correct photo next to each animal's name.

1. pygmy seahorses
2. Brazilian long-nosed bats
3. stone grasshopper
4. gray wolf
5. lion
6. European hares

A

B

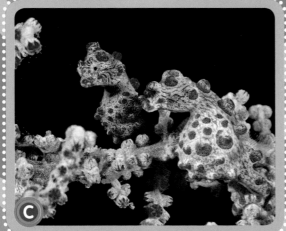

C

D

E

F

I SEE LONDON ...

These photos show close-up and faraway views of things in London, England. Unscramble the letters to identify what's in each picture.

Bonus: Use the highlighted letters to figure out the puzzle below.

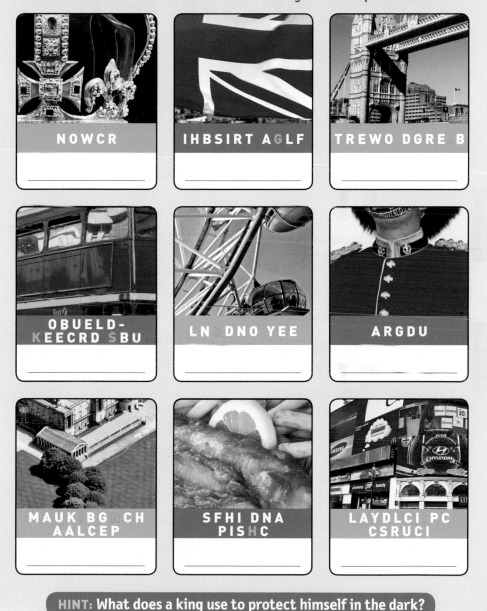

NOWCR

_____

IHBSIRT AGLF

_____

TREWO DGRE B

_____

OBUELD-
KEECRD SBU

_____

LN DNO YEE

_____

ARGDU

_____

MAUK BGN CH
AALCEP

_____

SFHI DNA
PISHC

_____

LAYDLCI PC
CSRUCI

_____

HINT: What does a king use to protect himself in the dark?

ANSWER: ___ N ___ ___ ___ T ___ V ___ ___

Mind Your Manners

1 In Chile, which is the preferred method for eating french fries?

a. eating them with a knife and fork
b. eating them from a paper cone
c. eating them with lots of ketchup
d. eating them inside sandwiches and burgers

2 In traditional Korean dining, where would guests sit?

a. on the floor   c. on the sidewalk
b. at a round table   d. outdoors

3 True or false? In Japan, it is considered rude to stand your chopsticks up in your rice bowl.

4 The Continental style of dining favored by Europeans means what?

a. Plates are in the different shapes of continents.
b. A fork is held in your left hand and a knife in your right.
c. All meals are eaten outdoors.
d. Dining guests are expected to name all continents before getting dessert.

5 What does the book *Emily Post's Table Manners for Kids* advise about texting when dining?

a. It is perfectly acceptable.
b. It is acceptable if the host is also texting.
c. It is acceptable to text once dessert is served.
d. It is never acceptable to text during a meal.

6 What do Bedouins in the Middle East do to signal that they do not want more coffee?

a. put a chair on the table
b. shake a cup
c. shout "Enough!"
d. wink three times

7 Which food did early Greeks give guests as a symbol of hospitality?

a. olives
b. bananas
c. Greek salad
d. salt

8 If a German host calls out "Guten Appetit!" before you eat, what is the host saying to you?

a. "May your gut be filled with good food."
b. "German food is yummy."
c. "Enjoy your meal!"
d. "Rub-a-dub-dub, here comes the grub!"

9 True or false? Loudly slurping soup in Japan is an offense that carries a hefty fine.

10 Which custom is common to many parts of Asia, Africa, and the Middle East but not to Europe and the United States?

a. singing at the table
b. eating with your hands
c. not speaking at the table
d. eating dessert first

11 In South India, you should never touch your plate with what?

a. your fork
b. your neighbor's elbow
c. a shoe
d. your left hand

Powers of Nature

1 According to popular legend, how was the Great Chicago Fire started?

a. A cow kicked over a lantern.
b. Lightning hit a lumberyard.
c. A coal mine exploded.
d. A backyard barbecue got seriously out of control.

2 Which technology was first used to track weather during World War II?

a. weather balloon
b. radar
c. thermometer
d. anemometer

3 Which type of natural disaster took place in Fukushima, Japan, in 2011?

a. a gravity wave
b. a hurricane
c. an earthquake
d. a zombie outbreak

4 Which city was buried when Mount Vesuvius in Italy erupted in A.D. 79?

a. Venice
b. Pompeii
c. New York
d. Hogsmeade

5 In March 1942, the most rain ever recorded in one month fell in Maui, Hawaii, U.S.A. How much of the wet stuff did they get?

a. 1 foot (30 cm)
b. 9 feet (3 m)
c. 15 feet (4.5 m)
d. 30 feet (9 m)

6 In the 1940s, which of these places was a new spot for surfers looking to catch some waves in the winter?

a. Lake Michigan
b. Mississippi River
c. Black Sea
d. Nile River

SURFER

7 In 2010, the world's largest known hailstone was measured to be the size of a _____.

a. tomato
b. softball
c. volleyball
d. watermelon

8 A rare fire rainbow was spotted in Scotland in July 2012, lasting only _____ before it disappeared.

a. 5 seconds
b. 20 seconds
c. 5 minutes
d. 20 minutes

9 Which of the following was NOT the name of a major hurricane to hit the United States?

a. Katrina
b. Wallis
c. Ike
d. Rita

FIRE RAINBOW

10 **True or false?** Iraq's 2009 sandstorm lasted almost two days.

11 Waterspouts sometimes pick up animals and then "rain" them down. Animals that have fallen from the sky have included fish, worms, and _____.

a. poodles
b. eagles
c. frogs
d. unicorns

WATERSPOUT

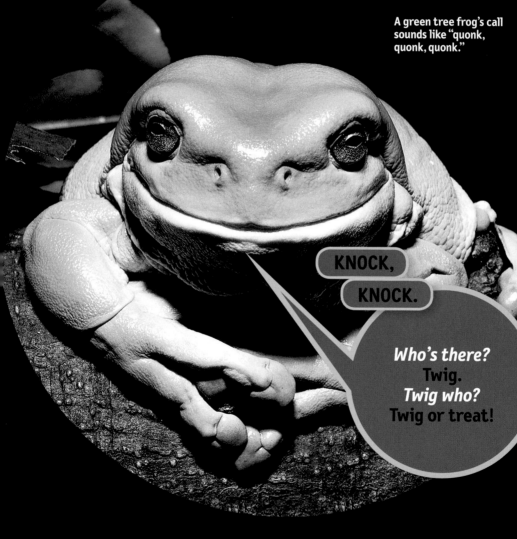

A green tree frog's call sounds like "quonk, quonk, quonk."

KNOCK, KNOCK.

Who's there?
Twig.
Twig who?
Twig or treat!

THINK PINK

These photographs show close-up and faraway views of pink things. Unscramble the letters to identify each picture. Bonus: Use the highlighted letters to solve the puzzle below.

LMAIGSOFN

OHT-IAR OLABONL

NGDHUTUO

SWMOR

UONEGT

RHATEFE

DDYIATK

TASCYRL

EHRSSOAE

HINT: This treat is sticky and sweet, but when it's done, it could end up on your feet.

ANSWER: B _ _ _ B _ _ _ _ _

103

Movie GREATS

SNOW WHITE AND DWARFS

1 In the classic Disney movie *Snow White and the Seven Dwarfs*, which of the following is *not* one of the seven dwarfs?
a. Sleepy
b. Happy
c. Grumpy
d. Lazy

2 The movie *E.T.: The Extra-Terrestrial* is about a boy who tries to help a space alien named E.T. Why does E.T. need help?
a. He's stranded on Earth and wants to go home.
b. He wants to learn how to ride a bike.
c. He wants to take control of Earth.
d. He needs to come up with a good Halloween costume.

E.T.

3 Which snack was first served in movie theaters in 1912?
a. hot dogs
b. Milk Duds
c. popcorn
d. Junior Mints

4 To watch 3-D movies in the 1950s, people wore glasses that had two colored filters. What were the colors?
a. black and orange
b. pink and purple
c. blue and red
d. green and brown

5 What is the title of the book that the movie *Willy Wonka & the Chocolate Factory* is based on?
a. *Willy Wonka and the Chocolate Factory*
b. *Charlie and the Chocolate Factory*
c. *Veruca Salt and the Chocolate Factory*
d. *Violet and the Chocolate Factory*

6 In the Indiana Jones movies, Dr. Henry "Indiana" Jones travels around the world searching for lost or mysterious objects. What is his job?
a. pediatrician
b. archaeologist
c. paleontologist
d. zookeeper

7 Which movie was *not* part of The Lord of the Rings trilogy?
a. *The Fellowship of the Ring*
b. *Attack of the Clones*
c. *The Two Towers*
d. *The Return of the King*

GANDALF FROM THE LORD OF THE RINGS TRILOGY

MUFASA WITH
CUB SIMBA IN
THE LION KING

8 **True or false?** The Nickel-odeon television network is named after the first cartoon character that ever appeared on the network.

9

In *The Lion King*, Simba is rescued and raised by ___.

a. a group of hyenas
b. an elephant
c. humans
d. a meerkat and a warthog

10 **Which famous cartoon character first appeared in the 1928 short movie *Steamboat Willy*?**

a. Mickey Mouse
b. Bart Simpson
c. Bugs Bunny
d. Fred Flintstone

11 In *The Wizard of Oz*, Dorothy Gale lived on a farm located where?

a. Oz
b. Kansas, U.S.A.
c. Emerald City
d. Cancún, Mexico

12 **The word "Supercalifragilisticexpialidocious" comes from which movie about an unusual nanny (shown above)?**

a. *Nanny McPhee*
b. *Mrs. Doubtfire*
c. *Mary Poppins*
d. *Daddy Day Care*

13 **Which classic movie made people afraid to go in the ocean?**

a. *March of the Penguins*
b. *Finding Nemo*
c. *Jaws*
d. *Free Willy*

KEIKO AND JESSE
IN *FREE WILLY*

Perfect Match

Nine sets of identical twins and one set of triplets go to Camp Double Take. Find the look-alike(s) for each numbered camper. Hint: The clothing for the correct matches is identical, but some of the kids are wearing different sports gear.

GIRLS' SHOWERS

We Gave It a Swirl

Use the clues below to figure out which animals appear in these swirled pictures.

1

HINT! A movie starring this clown did swimmingly at the box office.

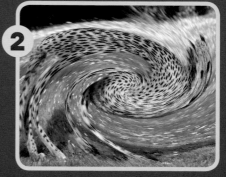

2

HINT! If this sprinter took off down a highway, it could run fast enough to get a speeding ticket.

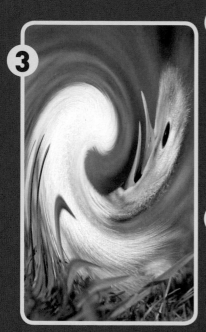

3

HINT! Hey, who are you calling a quack?

4

HINT! Slowing down climate change can help protect animals like this Arctic giant.

5

HINT! This many-legged creature will go through a major transformation.

SAVE OUR SHIP!

Strange things are happening on this cruise ship, and the guests are sending out an **SOS!** Help them figure out the three-word phrase that describes each of the numbered scenes. The first and last words always begin with **s**, and the middle word always begins with **o**. For example, the answer to number one is "Sailor operates saw." Ready to abandon ship?

Just Joking

Parrots eat seeds, nuts, and fruit. Some parrots can live for 80 years or more!

KNOCK, KNOCK.

Who's there?
Paul.
Paul who?
Paul up a chair and I will tell you.

Ready, Set, Eat!

These neighbors have gathered for a Thanksgiving potluck dinner, but all the food has gone missing from the kitchen. Find the 15 items on the list so the guests can enjoy their meal.

1. baked potato
2. green beans
3. roast turkey
4. carrots
5. pumpkin pie
6. cauliflower
7. mushrooms
8. cranberry sauce
9. gravy
10. corn
11. apple
12. baguette
13. Brussels sprouts
14. bell peppers
15. asparagus

Doggone FUN!

1 The smallest adult dog on record was a member of which breed?
- **a.** poodle
- **b.** Chihuahua
- **c.** Newfoundland
- **d.** miniature schnauzer

2 **True or false?** Dalmatian puppies are born with all the spots they will ever have.

3 **True or false?** Almost all adult dogs have about 320 bones and 42 permanent teeth.

TEACUP POODLE

4 What percentage of dog owners have admitted to signing their pets' names on greeting cards sent from the family?
- **a.** 91 percent
- **b.** 12 percent
- **c.** 2 percent
- **d.** Zero ... that's ridiculous!

5 The African basenji is also called the barkless dog. What does this dog do instead of barking?
- **a.** It hums.
- **b.** It uses sign language.
- **c.** It yodels.
- **d.** It doesn't make a sound.

AFRICAN BASENJI

6 About how long does it take to train a Seeing Eye dog?
- **a.** 3 days
- **b.** 2 weeks
- **c.** 4 months
- **d.** 36 months

7 Which country has the highest dog population?
a. Venezuela
b. Egypt
c. France
d. the United States

8 Which are the most popular names for male dogs in English-speaking countries?
a. Rover and Fido
b. Phineas and Ferb
c. Max and Buddy
d. Batman and Robin

9 Giant George has his own Facebook page and had a book written about him. What made Giant George so famous?
a. He was the world's shortest dog.
b. He was the world's fastest dog.
c. He was the world's tallest dog.
d. He could update his own Facebook page.

GIANT GEORGE

10 Three dogs—two Pomeranians and a Pekingese—should probably all have been named Lucky. What did these three dogs survive?
a. obedience school
b. the sinking of the *Titanic*
c. a tsunami
d. getting lost at a cat show

11 Reaching speeds up to 45 miles an hour (72 km/h), what breed of dog is the fastest on Earth?
a. Chihuahua
b. Australian shepherd
c. Rhodesian ridgeback
d. greyhound

12 An Australian cattle dog named Bluey is the longest living dog on record. How long did Bluey live?
a. 3 years and 2 months
b. 19 years and 11 months
c. 29 years and 5 months
d. 45 years

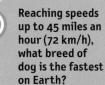
AUSTRALIAN CATTLE DOG

Dinner Party in the U.S.A.

The shapes of 15 states are hidden in this Thanksgiving dinner scene. Use the map (top left) to help you find and circle them. **BONUS:** Name each of the 15 hidden states.

NOVEMBER

114

Just Joking

Sea otter

KNOCK,
KNOCK.

Who's there?
Juicy.
Juicy who?
Juicy what I
just saw?

Funny List

Advice for a turkey on Thanksgiving:

1. Disguise yourself as broccoli and stand next to the pie.
2. Say you're too chicken to show up for dinner.
3. Stop waddling and start running.
4. Take a European vacation.

Q Did you hear about the ice that got fired?

A It was crushed.

Q Why did they let the turkey join the band?

A Because he had the drumsticks.

115

ANCIENT EGYPT

1 To make a **mummy**, ancient Egyptians removed all the organs from the body except the ____.

a. brain
b. heart
c. lungs
d. liver

2 Which one of the following was *not* a **ruler** of ancient Egypt?

a. Tutankhamun
b. Cleopatra
c. Attila the Hun
d. Nefertiti

3 The **Great Sphinx** of Giza—an ancient statue that still exists today—has the head of a human and the body of what animal?

a. cow
b. horse
c. pig
d. lion

4 What is the ancient Egyptian writing system called?

a. Egyptographs
b. cursive
c. katakana
d. hieroglyphic

5 True or false? Some ancient Egyptians mummified their pets.

6 What title did many Egyptian rulers use?

a. pharaoh
b. tsar
c. prime minister
d. emperor

7 Ancient Egyptians associated **which animal** with the gods?

a. cat
b. rabbit
c. rattlesnake
d. crocodile

PYRAMIDS AT GIZA

8 **True or false?** Rulers weren't allowed to show their hair in public.

9 **It took about 30,000 workers to build the Great Pyramid at Giza.** How long did it take them to build this pyramid?

a. 5 years
b. 10 years
c. 40 years
d. 80 years

10 **King Tutankhamun** was only nine years old when he became Egypt's ruler. How old was Tut when he died?

a. 10
b. 19
c. 35
d. 50

11 Which **dog breed** was often used as a hunting dog in Ancient Egypt?

a. poodle
b. greyhound
c. golden retriever
d. Scottish terrier

12 **True or false?** **Men wore makeup** in ancient Egypt.

13 **The ancient Egyptian civilization was built around what river?**

a. Amazon
b. Nile
c. Tiber
d. Danube

14 **The scarab** was a sacred insect in ancient Egypt. What is a scarab?

a. a mosquito
b. a dung beetle
c. a scorpion
d. an ant

15 **True or false?** **All Egyptian mummies were buried inside tombs.**

THE HOLE THING

These photographs show close-up views of things with holes. Unscramble the letters to identify what's in each picture.

Bonus: Use the highlighted letters to solve the puzzle below.

GUTONDHU
_____

SISWS ESHECE
_____

TRGAIU
_____

IBRATB LEOH
_____

NERNI EUTB
_____

YEKEOHL
_____

RALCEE
_____

NEMOCBOHY
_____

FOLG OELH
_____

HINT: It's great for a golfer, but not for a pair of pants.

ANSWER: ___ ___ O ___ ___ ___ ___ ___ ___

Just Joking

KNOCK, KNOCK.

Who's there?
Noah.
Noah who?
Noah good place for dinner? I'm starving!

Cats use their whiskers to "feel" whether they will fit into a space they are entering.

119

ANIMAL Speak

1 When a bee finds food, it alerts other bees to its location by ____.
   a. dancing
   b. purring
   c. buzzing
   d. barking

2 Cheetahs communicate with lots of noises, but which one of these sounds will you *never* hear a cheetah make?
   a. purr
   b. hiss
   c. growl
   d. roar

3 What would an ant do to express "Danger ahead!"?
   a. secrete chemicals
   b. run toward water
   c. roll on its back
   d. squeal

4 How do elephants greet each other?
   a. swat each other with their tails
   b. run around in circles
   c. butt heads
   d. entwine their trunks

5 What are some sounds that dolphins use to communicate?
   a. whistles
   b. squeaks
   c. clicks
   d. all of the above

6 **True or false?** Carnivorous fish called piranhas can bark.

BOTTLENOSE DOLPHIN

PIRANHA

NORTHERN
SAW-WHET OWL

7 Which of the following is *not* a form of wolf communication?

a. howling
b. scent secretions
c. body language
d. mooing

8 To attract a mate, owls may _____.

a. sing
b. sleep
c. dance
d. howl

9 **True or false?** Snakes stick out their tongues to communicate with each other.

10 A lion's roar can be heard miles away. The roar most likely tells other lions:

a. "This is *my* piece of land!"
b. "Come over and play!"
c. "I'm so bored."
d. "Let's find an antelope to pick on."

11 **True or false?** Zebras may use their unique stripes to help identify each other.

12 What does an adult male walrus use the air pouch in its throat for?

a. as a pillow
b. to sing
c. to call out female walruses
d. to blow bubbles

PACIFIC
WALRUS

MAP MANIA!
You Saw It Here First

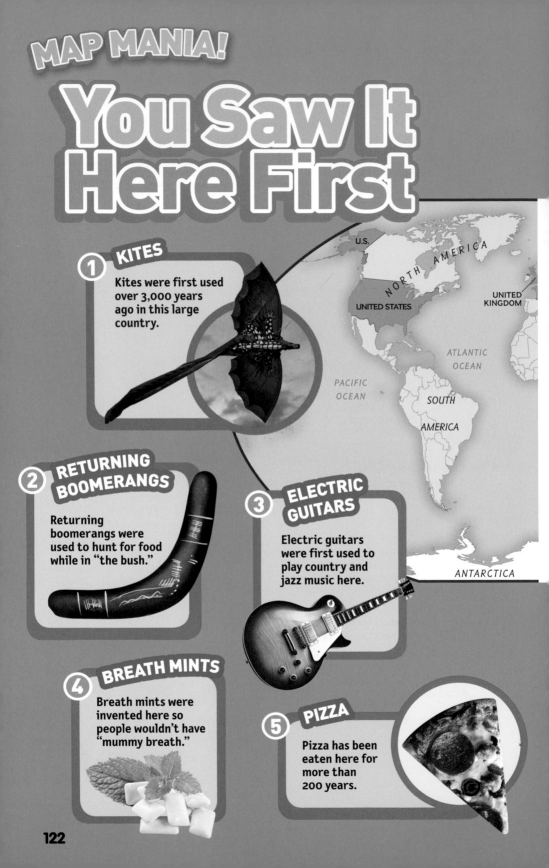

1 KITES
Kites were first used over 3,000 years ago in this large country.

2 RETURNING BOOMERANGS
Returning boomerangs were used to hunt for food while in "the bush."

3 ELECTRIC GUITARS
Electric guitars were first used to play country and jazz music here.

4 BREATH MINTS
Breath mints were invented here so people wouldn't have "mummy breath."

5 PIZZA
Pizza has been eaten here for more than 200 years.

U.S.

NORTH AMERICA

UNITED STATES

UNITED KINGDOM

ATLANTIC OCEAN

PACIFIC OCEAN

SOUTH AMERICA

ANTARCTICA

Every day, people use things that were invented in different parts of the world. For each invention, match the number to the country where it was invented.

⑥ FLUSHING TOILETS

The first flushing toilets were found in the "water closets" here.

⑦ VELCRO

The idea of Velcro came from an engineer who found burrs stuck to his jacket while hunting in this country.

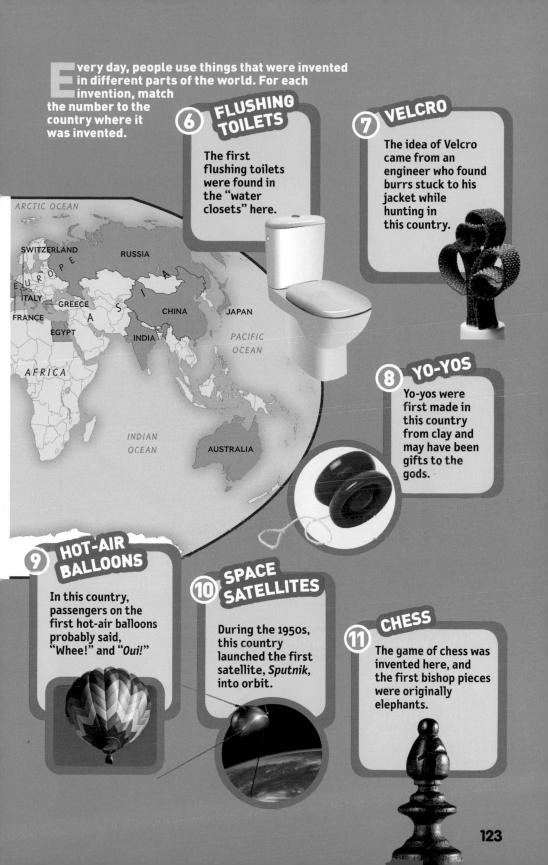

ARCTIC OCEAN

SWITZERLAND
RUSSIA
EUROPE
ITALY — GREECE
FRANCE
CHINA
JAPAN
ASIA
EGYPT
INDIA
PACIFIC OCEAN

AFRICA

INDIAN OCEAN

AUSTRALIA

⑧ YO-YOS

Yo-yos were first made in this country from clay and may have been gifts to the gods.

⑨ HOT-AIR BALLOONS

In this country, passengers on the first hot-air balloons probably said, "Whee!" and "*Oui!*"

⑩ SPACE SATELLITES

During the 1950s, this country launched the first satellite, *Sputnik*, into orbit.

⑪ CHESS

The game of chess was invented here, and the first bishop pieces were originally elephants.

Just Joking

**KNOCK,
KNOCK.**

Who's there?
Who.
Who who?
Hey, that's
my line!

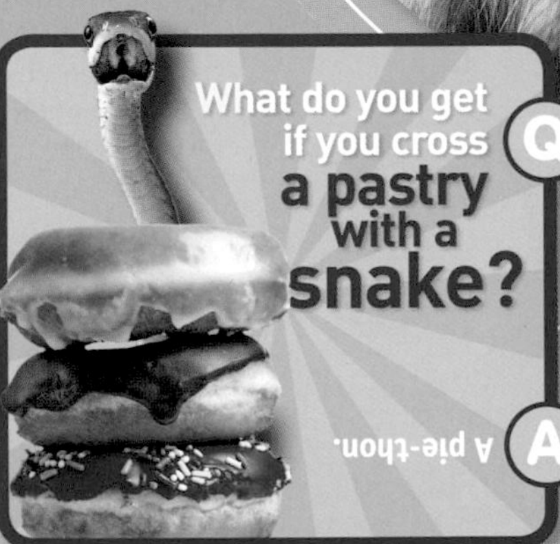

What do you get
if you cross
a pastry
with a
snake?

Q

A A pie-thon.

TONGUE TWISTER!

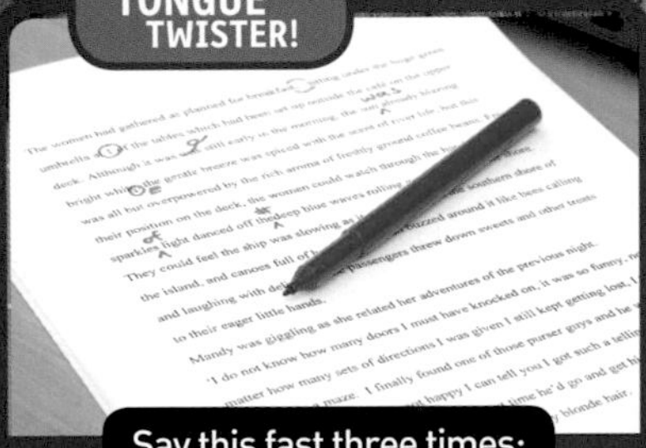

Say this fast three times:

Eddie edited it.

You've **got** to be joking ...

Q What did the
cherries
do with the
treasure?

A They berried it on
a dessert island.

SAfaRi racE

By now you know cheetahs are fast—but how fast is fast? Can this cheetah beat a safari jeep to the finish line? Get with a pal to finish this maze. And no cheet-ing!

Start

Finish

Traveling CIRCUS

1 About how fast does a human cannonball fly through the air?
- **a.** 20 miles an hour (32 km/h)
- **b.** 30 miles an hour (48 km/h)
- **c.** 70 miles an hour (113 km/h)
- **d.** 100 miles an hour (161 km/h)

2 What food do circus performers consider bad luck and never eat before a performance?
- **a.** peanuts
- **b.** popcorn
- **c.** hot dogs
- **d.** pretzels

3 What might circus performers keep in their pockets because it is good luck?
- **a.** turtle's foot
- **b.** elephant hair
- **c.** tiger's tail
- **d.** horse's mane

4 What is the average size of a clown's shoe?
- **a.** 10
- **b.** 14
- **c.** 18EE
- **d.** 26EEEE

5 Vivian Wheeler is famous for what facial feature?
- **a.** big red nose
- **b.** one large hairy eyebrow
- **c.** most number of freckles
- **d.** 11-inch (28-cm) beard

6 This nickname will make your skin crawl! Even though they love them, what do circus performers call their fans?
- **a.** circus spiders
- **b.** lot lice
- **c.** fan fleas
- **d.** clapping ants

7 Everybody loves the circus! What U.S. president traveled to Philadelphia to see the first American circus?

a. Alexander Hamilton
b. John F. Kennedy
c. Franklin D. Roosevelt
d. George Washington

8 True or false? For good luck, circus performers always jump into the ring with both feet.

9 A Frenchman, Jules Leotard, strung cords and a bar over a swimming pool in 1859 and invented what circus act?

a. juggling
b. clowning
c. flying trapeze
d. tightrope walk

CIRCUS PERFORMERS

10 True or false? Bozo the Clown, a popular TV show character during the 1960s, was not one clown, but many different actors playing the character.

11 What will get a circus performer sent out of a dressing room and forced to turn around three times before being allowed back in?

a. whistling
b. crying
c. singing
d. talking

12 What is considered to bring bad luck during a circus parade?

a. waving to the crowd
b. looking backward
c. shaking hands
d. signing autographs

13 Which U.S. president declared National Clown Week to be the first week of August?

a. Richard Nixon
b. Barack Obama
c. Herbert Hoover
d. Thomas Jefferson

14 Sore throats were probably common among performers in which country, where sword swallowing began thousands of years ago?

a. Mexico
b. Canada
c. Norway
d. India

What in the World?

GOING GLOBAL

These photographs show views of world landmarks. Unscramble the letters to identify what's in each picture. **Bonus:** Use the highlighted letters to solve the puzzle below.

UATSET FO REIYLBT
_____

TNEN HGESO
_____

DELGON ATEG EIBDRG
_____

A TGER LALW FO AICNH
_____

IGB ENB
_____

LFEE F WRT OE
_____

ACMUH IPCUCH
_____

JAT AALHM
_____

NIXHPS
_____

HINT: This U.S. landmark is made of 45-foot-tall vowels and consonants.

ANSWER: _____ _____ Y _ O O _ _____

Just Joking

The caracal is an excellent acrobat. It can leap high into the air and catch a bird in flight!

KNOCK, KNOCK.

Who's there?
Myth.
Myth who?
I myth you too!

129

Slithery Slimy Search!

Uh oh! Someone freed all the snakes, frogs, lizards, and turtles in the reptile/amphibian exhibit at the zoo! See if you can find the following creepy crawlies to put them back where they belong:

2	turtles
12	snakes
17	frogs
10	lizards

Not ready for the fun to end? Can you find these bonus items?

9 things that have yellow on them
4 things partly hidden under the leaves
4 gummy snakes
3 snakes sticking out their tongues
25 things with tails

Help the bottlenose dolphin mother and baby swim to the family reunion. Only one path through the sea will let them join the big family get-together!

finiSh

staRt

TREASURE HUNT

This explorer has discovered an ancient city in the jungle. Help her find these items hidden in this secret world.

1. diamonds
2. gold coins
3. monkey statue
4. rock art
5. bow and arrow
6. treasure map
7. treasure chest
8. crown
9. drum
10. cave opening

DANGER! QUICKSAND!

BE POLITE AROUND THE GLOBE

1 If you want **to greet** someone in **Tibet,** you can ____.

a. stick out your tongue
b. brush your hair
c. spin around
d. scream

2 In **England,** people often do this when they don't like a performer.

a. clap slowly
b. laugh
c. whistle
d. stay in their seats

3 It is customary for people in **Morocco** to offer their guests what?

a. mint tea
b. handmade rugs
c. pine nuts
d. camels

4 In **Bulgaria,** which of these gestures means "yes"?

a. nodding your head
b. shaking your head
c. smiling
d. running in place

5 In the **Czech Republic,** what do wedding guests often throw at a newly married couple?

a. rice
b. peas
c. flowers
d. rocks

6 In **Japan,** what is it polite to do before entering someone's house?

a. knock on the door three times
b. put on a hat
c. take off your shoes
d. jump up and down

7 In **Holland,** it is polite to eat your bread in what way?

a. with your hands
b. with chopsticks
c. with a knife and fork
d. with your feet

8 In **Indonesia,** what body part should you use to point to something?

a. thumb
b. elbow
c. index finger
d. foot

9 People in Switzerland think it's gross to do what in public?

a. speak
b. hold hands
c. chew gum
d. kiss

10 True or false? In **China,** it is considered **rude** to eat everything on your plate.

11 True or false? In **Turkey,** a strong handshake is considered impolite.

12 What number is considered lucky in **Italy?**

a. 3
b. 7
c. 13
d. 21

13 In what country is it **rude** to **make eye** contact when you greet someone?

a. Spain
b. Denmark
c. United States
d. China

14 In **Taiwan,** it's polite to do what if you enjoyed your meal?

a. rub your belly
b. smile
c. burp
d. take a nap

Just Joking

Q What did the deck of cards order for lunch?

A A club sandwich.

Merino sheep originated in Spain and are known for producing fine wool.

Where did the **sheep** get its hair cut?

At the baa-baa shop.

136

Q What is the elephant's favorite vegetable?

A Squash.

Q Which hand would you use to pick up a dangerous snake?

A Someone else's.

A police officer saw a woman in her car with a penguin. The officer said, "It's against the law to have that penguin in your car! Take it to the zoo."

The next day the police officer saw the same woman in her car with the same penguin. He said, "I told you to take that penguin to the zoo!"

The woman replied, "I did. He liked it so much, today we're going to the beach!"

Q What do you call **a grizzly bear** with **no teeth?**

A A gummy bear.

Undersea Skiing

These sea creatures have gathered from all over the world to vacation at this undersea ski lodge. Join the fun by finding the 15 items below.

1. treasure chest
2. inner tube
3. scarf
4. book
5. earmuffs
6. pail
7. sand castle
8. scuba mask
9. playing cards
10. carrot
11. cookies
12. hot cocoa
13. postcard
14. chandelier
15. sled

KNOCK, KNOCK.

Who's there?
Isabel.
Isabel who?
Isabel working?
I've been ringing
it for hours.

This tropical rainbow toucan sleeps by folding its tail over its head and resting its long bill over its back.

Wonders of NATURE

1 **What is the fastest growing plant on Earth, growing about 35 inches (91 cm) a day?**

a. kudzu vine
b. bamboo
c. spider plant
d. dandelion

2 **The oldest individual tree on Earth is a bristlecone pine. About how old is it?**

a. 100 years old
b. 586 years old
c. 5,062 years old
d. 1.5 million years old

3 **The world's largest beaver dam is so big, it can be located using Google Earth. How big is it?**

a. two times the length of Hoover Dam
b. three times the length of a tennis court
c. five times the size of a bathtub
d. the same size as Yankee Stadium in New York

4 **One of the world's largest spiderwebs was found in Texas, U.S.A. About how big was it?**

a. the size of two football fields
b. the size of two extra-large pizzas with mosquito toppings
c. the size of Loch Ness
d. the size of the Great Wall of China

5 **The convergent ladybug can have 13 of these. What are they?**

a. pairs of legs
b. eyes
c. layers of wings
d. spots

6 **True or false? Electric eels generate enough electricity to light up a Christmas tree.**

7 What is Earth's loudest animal?

a. the screech owl
b. the elephant
c. the blue whale
d. the laughing hyena

8 True or false? Some species of seals can hold their breath underwater for an hour.

9 About how many glasses of milk can the average cow produce in its lifetime?

a. 240
b. 720
c. 700,000
d. 200,000

10 How big was the world's largest jack-o'-lantern?

a. 24 pounds (11 kg)
b. 200 pounds (91 kg)
c. 1,811 pounds (821 kg)
d. 2,345 pounds (1,064 kg)

12 About how many quills does a porcupine have?

a. 700   b. 1,400
c. 10,000   d. 30,000

11 How fast can a woodpecker peck?

a. 20 times a second
b. 150 times a second
c. 300 times a second
d. 850 times a second

HEART-TO-HEART

These photographs show close-up and faraway views of heart-shaped things. Unscramble the letters to identify what's in each picture. Bonus: Use the highlighted letters to solve the puzzle below.

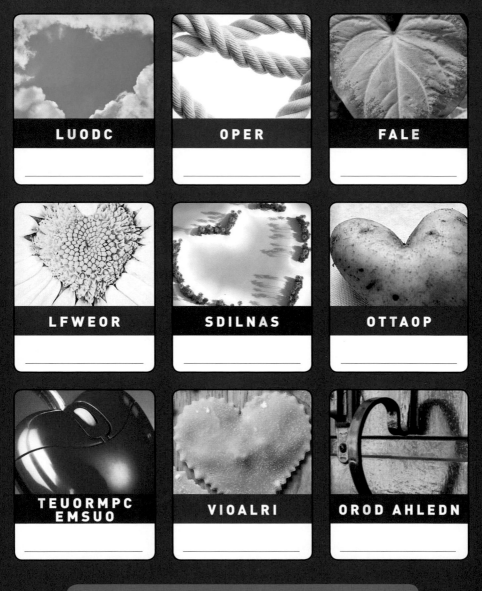

LUODC

OPER

FALE

LFWEOR

SDILNAS

OTTAOP

TEUORMPC EMSUO

VIOALRI

OROD AHLEDN

HINT: How do you interrupt a candy conversation heart?

ANSWER: Y ___ ___ ___ ___ ___ ___ ___ ___ .

142

Just Joking

I'll take mine to go! Mandrills have large pockets in their cheeks that they stuff with food to eat at a later time.

KNOCK, KNOCK.

Who's there?
Ivana.
Ivana who?
Ivana go for a pizza; care to join me?

SPLASH**DOWN**

START!

enter

Body Parts

1 If you could line up all the blood vessels in the human body, they would be long enough to wrap around the world _____ times.

a. 2½
b. 4
c. 3½
d. 1

2 Some people with vision loss can improve their sight by using a tiny video camera mounted on their _____ that sends signals to their brain.

a. wristbands
b. necklaces
c. headbands
d. sunglasses

3 On average, a person's heart pumps enough blood every day to fill_____.

a. a milk carton
b. a swimming pool
c. a tanker truck
d. three supertanker ships

4 What does the medical term *rhinotillexomania* refer to? (Hint: The prefix *rhino-* refers to the nose.)

a. fascination with plastic surgery on the nose
b. obsessive nose picking
c. fear of rhinoceroses
d. an excessively large nose

5 What is the strongest muscle in the human body?

a. leg muscle
b. little toe
c. tongue
d. arm muscle

6 True or false? It's impossible to tickle yourself.

7 About how many bacteria are on each inch of the average person's skin?

a. 32 million
b. 1 million
c. 100,000
d. 700

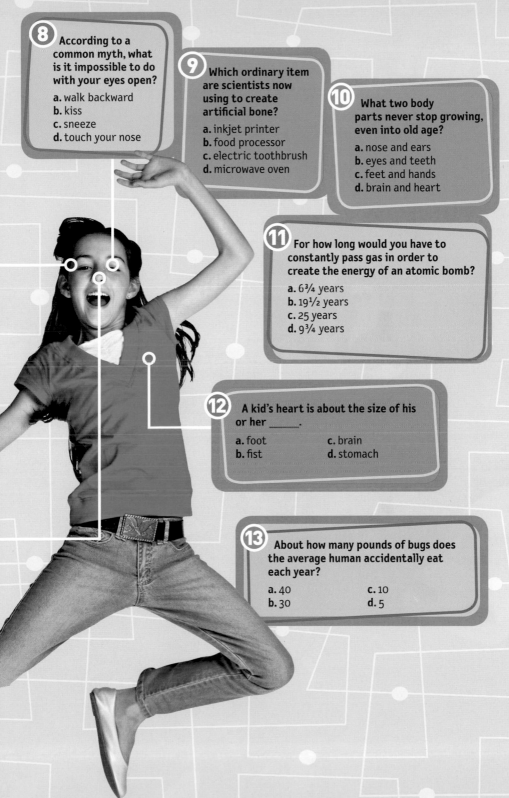

8 According to a common myth, what is it impossible to do with your eyes open?
a. walk backward
b. kiss
c. sneeze
d. touch your nose

9 Which ordinary item are scientists now using to create artificial bone?
a. inkjet printer
b. food processor
c. electric toothbrush
d. microwave oven

10 What two body parts never stop growing, even into old age?
a. nose and ears
b. eyes and teeth
c. feet and hands
d. brain and heart

11 For how long would you have to constantly pass gas in order to create the energy of an atomic bomb?
a. 6¾ years
b. 19½ years
c. 25 years
d. 9¾ years

12 A kid's heart is about the size of his or her _____.
a. foot
b. fist
c. brain
d. stomach

13 About how many pounds of bugs does the average human accidentally eat each year?
a. 40
b. 30
c. 10
d. 5

Get Spooked!

Real-life animals inspired many of the trick-or-treaters at this Halloween party. Find the 15 costumes listed below.

1. goblin shark
2. bumblebee bat
3. pink fairy armadillo
4. Gila monster
5. spider monkey
6. skeleton shrimp
7. leafy sea dragon
8. wolffish
9. milk snake
10. tiger mosquito
11. giraffe weevil
12. demon mole rat
13. vampire squid
14. spectacled bear
15. ghost frog

Just Joking

KNOCK,
KNOCK.

Who's there?
T. rex.
T. rex who?
Wait—a *T. rex* is at your
door and you want to
know its name?

CUSTOMER: There's a
dead beetle in my soup.
WAITER: Yes, sir,
they're not very
good swimmers.

TONGUE TWISTER!

Say this fast three times:

Girl gargoyle, guy gargoyle.

You've **got** to be joking ...

Q **What country did candy come from?**

A Sweeten.

Just Joking

HA! HA! HA! HA! HA! HA! HA! HA! HA! HA! HA! HA! HA! HA! HA! HA! HA!

The lesser hedgehog tenrec may look like a hedgehog, but it is actually not part of the hedgehog family.

KNOCK, KNOCK.

Who's there?
Meyer.
Meyer who?
Meyer nosy!

151

GREEK MYTHOLOGY

1 Where did **Greek Gods** supposedly live?

a. Mount Vesuvius
b. Mount St. Helens
c. Mount Everest
d. Mount Olympus

2 **Zeus**, king of the gods, is often shown with what weapon?

a. a lightning bolt
b. a fireball
c. a shield
d. a spear

3 In the Percy Jackson and the Olympians series, Percy learns that he is the son of **Poseidon**, god of the _____.

a. sea
b. trees
c. Earth
d. sky

4 The **Cyclops** is a Greek monster famous for having _____.

a. one eye
b. three ears
c. six legs
d. eight arms

5 **Medusa** is famous for having hair made of _____?

a. worms
b. snakes
c. octopus arms
d. eels

6 True or false? Everything **King Midas** touched turned to water.

7 Which present-day **Greek city** was named for Athena, the goddess of wisdom?

a. Ionia
b. Athens
c. Kalamata
d. Hydra

8 The **Trojan War,** described in a famous Greek epic, was fought over a beautiful woman named _____.

a. Aphrodite
b. Helen of Troy
c. Leda
d. Demeter

PARTHENON IN ATHENS, GREECE

9 Which god controlled the **underworld?**

a. Zeus
b. Hermes
c. Hades
d. Ares

10 **Artemis—** the goddess of the hunt—is often shown holding a _____.

a. jar of water
b. harp
c. bow and arrow
d. banana

11 True or false? **Aphrodite** was the queen of the gods.

12 **Achilles** was a powerful Greek hero who had only one weak spot on his body. What was it?

a. his elbow
b. his neck
c. his knee
d. his heel

Just Joking

Q

Why don't they serve **chocolate** in prison?

A Because it makes you break out.

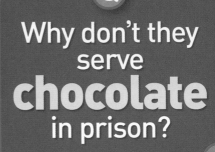

Q Why did Tony go out with a prune?

A Because he couldn't find a date.

TONGUE TWISTER!

Say this fast three times:

Bad money, mad bunny.

Q What do you call a borrowed bison?

A A buffa-loan.

FOR RENT

Q

Where can you **break a board** with your foot and then **sprinkle glitter** on it?

Martial arts and crafts class.

A

154

NATIONAL GEOGRAPHIC

ANIMAL JAM

Scout It Out

The Animal Jam characters want to explore Coral Canyon. Before they head out on their adventure, help them collect their camping gear.

1. backpack
2. compass
3. flashlight
4. map
5. sleeping bag
6. canteen
7. binoculars
8. lantern
9. walkie-talkie
10. first-aid kit
11. hiking boots
12. sunglasses
13. camera
14. climbing rope
15. skillet
16. bicycle

U.S. PRESIDENTS

1 Which president held office for the longest time?
a. Thomas Jefferson
b. Franklin D. Roosevelt
c. Richard Nixon
d. Bill Clinton

2 Eight U.S. presidents were born in this state, more than in any other state.
a. Massachusetts
b. Ohio
c. Virginia
d. Hawaii

3 All presidents had other careers before going into politics. Match the U.S. president to his former job.
a. actor
b. tailor
c. peanut farmer
d. baseball team owner
e. Andrew Johnson
f. Jimmy Carter
g. George W. Bush
h. Ronald Reagan

4 Who has been the tallest U.S. president to date?
a. George Washington
b. Thomas Jefferson
c. Abraham Lincoln
d. Barack Obama

5 **True or false?** George Washington had wooden teeth.

ABRAHAM LINCOLN

GEORGE WASHINGTON

6 The eighth president of the United States, Martin Van Buren, was nicknamed "Old Kinderhook." He was also known for creating which common expression? (Hint: Look at his nickname.)
a. LOL
b. OK
c. OMG
d. TMI

7 Before Theodore Roosevelt gave the White House its name in 1901, what had the president's home been called?
a. President's Palace
b. President's House
c. Executive Mansion
d. all of the above

BO THE PORTUGUESE
WATER DOG

(8) Match the name of the famous first pet to its presidential owner.
a. Sweetlips   e. Barack Obama
b. Bo   f. George Washington
c. King Tut   g. Ronald Reagan
d. Fuzzy   h. Herbert Hoover

(9) What is the U.S. president's yearly salary?
a. $100,000
b. $400,000
c. $750,000
d. $1,000,000

(10) **True or false?** Barack Obama is the first African American to be president of the United States.

(11) Known for his sweet tooth, Ronald Reagan kept a large jar of what kind of candy in the Oval Office?
a. M&M's
b. jelly beans
c. Sour Patch Kids
d. licorice

(12) Who was the first president to live in the White House?
a. George Washington
b. John Adams
c. James Madison
d. Thomas Jefferson

(13) Abraham Lincoln was known for wearing which type of clothing?
a. suspenders
b. top hat
c. sneakers
d. wristwatch

(14) What was usually on John F. Kennedy's lunch menu?
a. New England clam chowder
b. meat loaf
c. grilled cheese sandwich
d. hot dog

(15) What is the president's helicopter called?
a. Chopper One
b. Eagle One
c. Marine One
d. Flyer One

CHANGE YOUR STRIPES

These photographs show close-up views of stripes in the animal kingdom. Unscramble the letters to identify what's in each picture.

RGIET

_____

TSOPUOC

_____

ETBTYRULF

_____

HFJLYISEL

_____

LASIN

_____

NHAEELCOM

_____

RUETLT

_____

TMERIH ARBC

_____

ERZSAB

_____

Just Joking

This African leopard's spots, called rosettes, help it blend into its surroundings.

KNOCK, KNOCK.

Who's there?
Little old lady.
Little old lady who?
Hey, why are you yodeling?

MAP MANIA!
STILL STANDING

1 BIG BEN

The name "Big Ben" today often refers to the clock, tower, and bell. Which was the original Big Ben?
a. The Great Bell
b. The Great Clock
c. Elizabeth Tower
d. The King of England's friend, Ben.

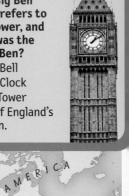

2 EIFFEL TOWER

True or false? When it was built in 1889, the Eiffel Tower was the tallest building in the world.

3 THE SPHINX

Why is the Sphinx missing its nose?
a. It was eroded by sandstorms.
b. It was destroyed by a person.
c. It was built without a nose.
d. It sneezed a little too hard.

4 LEANING TOWER OF PISA

True or false? The Leaning Tower of Pisa started leaning while it was being built.

NORTH AMERICA

BLARNEY, IRELAND

ATLANTIC OCEAN

PACIFIC OCEAN

SOUTH AMERICA

These famous structures have been around for quite a while! Test your knowledge about each cool construction and then match each one to its location.

THE KREMLIN

5 When it was first built, what was the Kremlin's original purpose?

a. a candy factory
b. a movie theater
c. a medieval fort
d. an amusement park

THE FORBIDDEN CITY

6 What was "forbidden" about the Forbidden City?

a. touching things
b. entering without permission
c. going to the bathroom
d. talking

BLARNEY CASTLE

7 Visitors to the Blarney Castle are encouraged to do what to the famous Blarney Stone?

a. write their name on it
b. kiss it
c. take it home
d. throw it at a leprechaun

8–14 MATCH EACH STRUCTURE TO ITS CORRECT LOCATION ON THE MAP.

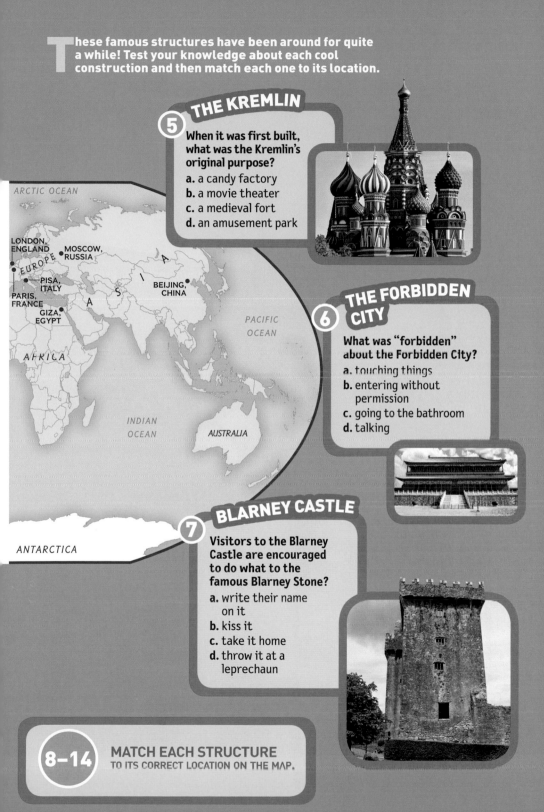

ARCTIC OCEAN

LONDON, ENGLAND
EUROPE
MOSCOW, RUSSIA
PISA, ITALY
PARIS, FRANCE
GIZA, EGYPT
AFRICA
ASIA
BEIJING, CHINA
PACIFIC OCEAN
INDIAN OCEAN
AUSTRALIA
ANTARCTICA

Just Joking

A Because it is stationery.

Q What kind of bird is always out of breath?

A A puffin.

TOURIST: I'd like to purchase a ticket to the moon, please.
TOUR GUIDE: Sorry, sir. The moon is full tonight.

CATHIE: Did your party guests enjoy the piñata?

DOUG: It was a huge hit!

A bearded dragon can change its skin color to deflect the sun and prevent overheating.

KNOCK, KNOCK.

Who's there?
Answer.
Answer who?
Answer all over the picnic basket!

MAP MANIA!
GREAT ADVENTURE

① ZAMBEZI RIVER

This wild river draws white-water rafters from all over the world. On what continent can it be found?

a. Africa
b. North America
c. Asia
d. South America

② ALASKA, U.S.A.

Which annual race covers more than a thousand miles (1,600 km) and crosses two mountain ranges in this U.S. state?

a. New York Marathon
b. Olympics
c. The Tour de France
d. Iditarod Sled Dog Race

③ ANTARCTICA

What animals might you see on a trip to this continent?

a. whales
b. penguins
c. seals
d. all of the above

④ GUADALUPE ISLAND, MEXICO

Thrill-seekers can view sharks from underwater cages off the coast of this island, located in what body of water?

a. Atlantic Ocean
b. Gulf of Mexico
c. Pacific Ocean
d. Red Sea

NORTH AMERICA

C

UNITED STATES

E

ECUADOR

A

ATLANTIC OCEAN

SOUTH AMERICA

PACIFIC OCEAN

Adventure-seekers travel the world to climb, dive, race, raft, and more! Find out how much you know about these thrilling adventures. Then match each adventure to the correct location on the map.

ARCTIC OCEAN

EUROPE

ASIA

AFRICA

B

PACIFIC OCEAN

INDIAN OCEAN

F

D
AUSTRALIA

E
ANTARCTICA

5 MOUNT EVEREST

Mountain climbers who want to conquer Mount Everest—the highest place on Earth—head to what Asian mountain range?
a. Andes
b. Canadian Rockies
c. Alps
d. Himalaya

6 AUSTRALIA

Cowboy types can saddle up for a nearly weeklong cattle drive across what rugged landscape in Australia?
a. Badlands
b. Outback
c. Never Go Back
d. Yukon

7 GALÁPAGOS ISLANDS

The Galápagos Islands, a popular spot for snorkelers, are located off the coast of what country?
a. Saudi Arabia
b. Ecuador
c. Mozambique
d. Cambodia

8–14 MATCH EACH OF THESE PLACES TO THE RED MARKER THAT SHOWS ITS CORRECT LOCATION ON THE MAP.

GOLD STANDARD

These photographs show close-up views of golden objects. Unscramble the letters to identify each picture. Bonus: Use the highlighted letters to solve the puzzle below.

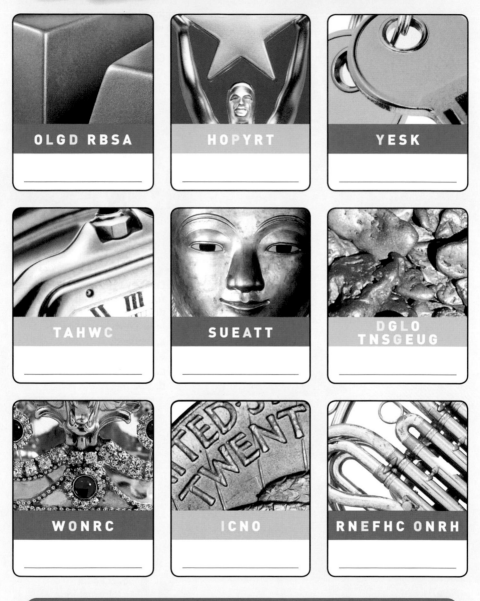

OLGD RBSA

HOPYRT

YESK

TAHWC

SUEATT

DGLO TNSGEUG

WONRC

ICNO

RNEFHC ONRH

HINT: You're the best in the world if you can win this every four years.

ANSWER: _ L _ M _ _ _ _ _ M _ _ _ _

166

NATIONAL GEOGRAPHIC

ANiMaL JaM ®

BONUS: Find 12 hearts in the scene.

Twinkle Toes

In February, the *Animal Jam* crew meets at the dance club to celebrate a holiday called Friendship Festival. Can you guess what each character is thinking? Fill in the number that matches the correct animal.

1. "Put your hands in the air like you just don't care!"
2. "Robots have nothing on me."
3. "Let's do the bunny hop!"
4. "Aloha! Let's hula!"
5. "My moves really pack in the crowds."
6. "Too much dancing—time for a catnap."
7. "It's time for the fox trot!"

AND NOW FOR MY NEXT TRICK...

1 From how far away can elephants still hear each other's low-rumbling calls?

a. 2 feet (.6 m)
b. 6 miles (10 km)
c. 81 miles (130 km)
d. 153 miles (246 km)

2 What trick can **hummingbirds** do?

a. fly upside down and backward
b. lift objects heavier than themselves
c. grow a new set of wings
d. make honey like bees

3 True or false? Crocodiles eat stones to help them grind and digest their food.

4 Which of the following is not a trick a **chameleon** can do?

a. move each of its eyes separately
b. change its color
c. hold its breath for several days
d. stretch its tongue longer than the size of its body

5 What crazy stunt does a **horned toad** perform when it feels threatened?

a. kick dirt at predators
b. shoot blood from its eyes
c. shoot poison from its tongue
d. change colors and hide

6 Which animal can grow up to **40 new** sets of teeth in its lifetime?

a. beaver
b. tarantula
c. alligator
d. snake

7 Each year, the purple frog (yes, it's really purple!) lives **above the ground** for only _____.

a. 2 days
b. 2 weeks
c. 5 weeks
d. 3 months

8 True or false? The deep-sea shrimp squirts its enemies with a glowing blue ooze.

9 Spitting spiders shoot a **sticky substance** at their prey to _____.

a. stun it
b. hold it down and eat it
c. blind it
d. add flavor

10 Which animal can change direction in midair while chasing its prey?

a. golden retriever
b. antelope
c. tabby cat
d. cheetah

11 How far can a **kangaroo leap?**

a. 3 feet (1 m)
b. 8 feet (2 m)
c. 44 feet (13 m)
d. 104 feet (32 m)

12 True or false? All spiders spin webs in the same pattern.

13 Which sea animal can dive over **6,600 feet** (2,010 m) below the surface of the water?

a. sperm whale
b. horseshoe crab
c. jellyfish
d. emperor penguin

Just Joking

Say this fast three times:

Russell wrangled wrestling rascals.

Q

Why did Dracula become a vegetarian?

A Because his doctor told him stake was bad for his heart.

KNOCK, KNOCK.

Who's there?
Kitten.
Kitten who?
You gotta be kitten me!

A kookaburra's call sounds like human laughter.

Mitten Mix-up

This park is full of wintry fun. But some people—and some *snow* people—are wearing the wrong mittens. Find and circle the ten matching pairs in this scene. (The white gloves don't count.)

HOT CIDER

Lost in

The Moon Rock concert just ended, but now these aliens can't find their spaceships in the parking lot. To help each alien locate its spaceship, follow these rules:

- Aliens with antennae need ships with pointed roofs.

- Short aliens need ladders to reach the doors of their ships.

- The number of windows on the spaceship must match the number of eyeballs on the alien.

- Purple aliens must return to the Purple Planet in purple spaceships.

THANKS for COMING!

EXIT

MOON-ROCK-A-THON!

Galaxy's Child
Moon tour
2004

space

1. ____

2. ____

A

5. ____

6. ____

4. ____

7. ____

173

Off the DEEP END

1 Tubeworms living near superhot vents eat what to survive?
   a. crabs boiled by the vents
   b. giant squid attracted to the vents
   c. poisonous gas spewing from the vents
   d. Krabby Patties from the nearest Krusty Krab

2 **True or false?** The blobfish, found at depths of more than 3,000 feet (914.4 m), has been voted the world's ugliest endangered creature.

BLOBFISH

3 Which of these is on the ocean floor and spans the entire planet?
   a. an underwater mountain range
   b. a very deep trench
   c. a coral reef
   d. a chain of starfish holding hands

4 If you were at the deepest point of the ocean, the weight of the water pushing down on you would feel most like _____.
   a. a person
   b. a car
   c. an airplane
   d. 50 airplanes

5 Besides making movies, James Cameron is also famous for doing what in the *DEEP SEA CHALLENGER* submersible?
   a. traveling to the ocean's darkest spot
   b. diving to the ocean's deepest point
   c. swimming in the coldest part of the ocean
   d. building the first underwater movie theater

DEEP SEA CHALLENGER

6 **True or false?** Cold salt water melting from sea ice can sink to the bottom of the ocean floor, creating a giant icicle as it sinks.

7 Spider crabs living on the ocean floor can grow up to how wide?

a. 1 foot (.3 m)
b. 3 feet (.9 m)
c. 12 feet (3.6 m)
d. 20 feet (6 m)

SPIDER CRAB

8 Scientists were shocked to discover that life on the ocean floor could exist without _____.

a. oxygen
b. food
c. gravity
d. Internet access

9 What did scientists discover on the ocean floor 1,000 miles (1,600 km) east of Japan?

a. the world's deepest canyon
b. the world's largest volcano
c. the world's tallest mountain
d. the world's largest Godzilla footprint

10 A deep-sea jellyfish will use flashy lights when attacked by a fish in order to _____.

a. scare the fish
b. blind the fish
c. attract a predator to eat the fish
d. convince the fish it was a lightbulb

11 What is the name given to the deepest part of the ocean?

a. Bikini Bottom
b. Mariana Trench
c. Champion Deep
d. Davy Jones's Locker

HELMET JELLY

GLOBAL GOBBLING

These photographs show close-up views of internationally inspired foods. Unscramble the letters to identify what's in each picture.
Bonus: Use the highlighted letters to solve the puzzle below.

ALGNIEB FWSLAEF

_____

IALNAIT CEI

_____

WDESSHI SELALTBMA

_____

ABNCU HNSDACIW

_____

AIZLRB USTN

_____

ERKGE AADLS

_____

SRULSBSE TRSOUPS

_____

SHENLGI IFMFNU

_____

ADP AITH

_____

HINT: A tightrope walker always eats this.

ANSWER: _ _ _ _ L _ _ B A _ A _ _ _ _ _ _ _

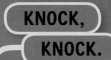

Just Joking

Ostriches are the world's largest birds.

KNOCK, KNOCK.

Who's there?
Isaiah.
Isaiah who?
Isaiah nothing until you open this door.

177

Bizarre Laboratory Tale

While this mad scientist eats a **b**acon, **l**ettuce, and **t**omato sandwich, his experiments are running wild. Each of the ten numbered experiments can be described with three words. The first word begins with **b**, the second with **l**, and the third with **t**. For example, the first experiment is "bunny lugs trophy." Can you figure out the nine others?

Just Joking

Most geckos have transparent eyelids that they keep clean with their tongues.

KNOCK, KNOCK.

Who's there?
Phillip.
Phillip who?
Phillip my bag with treats, please.

What in the World?

ALOHA SPIRIT

These photographs show close-up and faraway views of things you could see in Hawaii. Unscramble the letters to identify what's in each picture.

EPPIEPLSNA

_____

SELI

_____

TOCNCOU

_____

AIWAAHIN SIRHT

_____

ESA REUTLT

_____

NVLAOOC

_____

DAUSRFOBR

_____

EKUULLE

_____

IN YOUR BACKYARD

1 **Daisies** are found everywhere on Earth except _____.

a. Australia
b. Hawaii
c. Antarctica
d. Japan

2 True or false? **Dragonflies** can only see straight ahead.

3 True or false? Some **ladybugs** have stripes instead of spots.

4 **Squirrels** live all over the world except in which country?

a. Australia
b. Canada
c. England
d. Mexico

5 The American **robin** can roost in groups of how many in the winter?

a. 250
b. 2,500
c. 250,000
d. 2.5 million

6 What's the best way to **provide water** to birds?

a. in a bowl on the ground
b. in a bowl in a tree
c. in a water fountain
d. you should not give water to birds

7 A cricket's ears are located near its _____.

a. stomach
b. knees
c. eyes
d. mouth

8 A group of **mice** is called a _____.

a. gaggle
b. lot
c. swarm
d. mischief

9 At what temperature does **sand melt?**

a. 3ºF (16ºC)
b. 30ºF (-1ºC)
c. 300ºF (149ºC)
d. 3000ºF (1649ºC)

10 True or false? An **earthworm** can eat up to one-third its body weight in a day.

11 True or false? A **cockroach** can live for weeks **without its** head.

12 True or false? You can fry an **egg** on a very hot **sidewalk.**

13 How many **ants** live on Earth?

a. one million
b. one billion
c. one trillion
d. one quadrillion

14 What is the very **first thing** a caterpillar eats after it's born?

a. leaves
b. its own eggshell
c. other bugs
d. young caterpillars don't eat

SWALLOWTAIL CATERPILLAR

185

Q Why are sodas always so successful?

A Because they have a can-do attitude.

CUSTOMER: Waitress! Will my pancakes be long?

BAKER: No, sir, I expect they'll be round, as usual.

Which **dog** swims and **solves** mysteries?

Scuba Dooby Doo.

Go Fish!

Gil and his family are going on vacation. But first he has to run some errands. Find the route that gets him from his home to the entrances of the places on his list in order. He can't swim along the same path twice and can't pass the park or the bank's door.

TO DO:

1. RETURN BOOK TO LIBRARY
2. BUY SWIMSUIT AT MALL
3. PICK UP SUNSCREEN AT CONVENIENCE STORE
4. GET HAIRCUT
5. CATCH SUB

By the Numbers

1 If you attend school for 6 hours a day and 180 days a year, how many hours will you have been in school by the time you complete kindergarten to grade 12?

a. 84
b. 380
c. 14,040
d. Too many!

2 How many holes are there in a Wiffle ball?

a. 3: 2 for your fingers and 1 for your thumb
b. 8
c. 24
d. 120

3 In what year was Popeye the Sailor Man created?

a. 1899
b. 1929
c. 1945
d. 1990

POPEYE

4 How long is a bowling alley?

a. 3 feet (1 m)
b. 60 feet (18 m)
c. 200 feet (61 m)
d. 500 feet (152 m)

5 Which three numbers are used as the area code in telephone numbers in movies and television but not in real telephone numbers?

a. 222
b. 555
c. 845
d. 911

6 About how much does a million dollars weigh if it is all in one-dollar bills?

a. 1 pound (0.45 kg)
b. 500 pounds (228 kg)
c. 2,200 pounds (998 kg)
d. 1 million pounds (453,592 kg)

7 About how many times can you fold paper money before it tears?
a. 52
b. 257
c. 2,500
d. 4,000

8 **True or false?** It is 10:30 on the clock tower of Independence Hall pictured on the $100 bill issued in late 2013.

9 About how many slices of pizza are eaten each second in the U.S.?
a. 2
b. 15
c. 185
d. 350

10 About how many teeth can a shark lose over a lifetime?
a. fewer than 50
b. 100 to 200
c. 5,000 to 6,000
d. more than 30,000

11 Which country claims that over 99 percent of the adults living there have cell phones?
a. the United States
b. Great Britain
c. the Czech Republic
d. the nation of Cellphonia

12 How much does it cost to buy a bag of $10,000 in shredded money from the U.S. Bureau of Engraving and Printing?
a. Get the tape out. It's free!
b. $1.00
c. $45.00
d. $100.00

Just Joking

KNOCK,

KNOCK.

Who's there?
Thermos.
Thermos who?
Thermos be a
better knock-knock
joke than this.

190

A toucan does not have a large bill when it hatches; it takes a few months for its bill to become full size.

ORANGE OVERLOAD

These photographs show close-up views of things that are orange. Unscramble the letters to identify what's in each picture.
Bonus: Use the highlighted letters to solve the puzzle below.

KETBLALASB
_____

GRTEI
_____

ATROSCR
_____

LSVAEE
_____

RNOATGNUA
_____

RHNAMCO LETBFRUYT
_____

PNIUPMK
_____

ATPUNEOLAC
_____

ODIHFSLG
_____

HINT: This is a lumberjack's favorite month.

ANSWER: __ E __ __ – __ __ __ __ __ __ __ __

192

ANIMAL JAM

WELCOME TO JAMAA

Jammin' Jamaa

These characters from the virtual world of *Animal Jam* are exploring the town square of Jamaa. Find and circle at least ten things that don't belong in this scene. Hint: All of the animals are supposed to be there.

COOL CAVES

1 On average, how long does it take for most caves to get big enough for a person to fit inside?

a. about 10 years
b. about 100 years
c. about 1,000 years
d. about 100,000 years

2 These icicle-shaped formations form as water drips from the cave ceiling. What are they called?

a. stalagmites
b. stalactites
c. icicles
d. rocks

3 These pointy formations grow up from the floor where water drops fall. What are they called?

a. stalagmites
b. stalactites
c. totems
d. chopsticks

4 **True or false?** All bats sleep in caves.

5 Until 1986, miners took what animal with them into caves to test if the air was breathable?

a. dogs
b. cats
c. snakes
d. canaries

6 Which of these creatures often lives in caves?

a. glowworm
b. ostrich
c. cow
d. elephant

7 When stalactites and stalagmites touch, they can form what kind of structure?

a. a column
b. a big rock
c. a waterfall
d. an ice pillar

8 The world's largest cave is located where?

a. Kentucky, U.S.A.
b. Venice, Italy
c. Cairo, Egypt
d. Antarctica

10 What do you call a person who studies caves?
a. a caveologist
b. a speleologist
c. an entomologist
d. a rock-and-roller

9 Because there is no light, fish that live in caves are often _____.
a. blind
b. deaf
c. small
d. hungry

11 Carlsbad Caverns, pictured here, is located where?
a. Toledo, Spain
b. Tulum, Mexico
c. Whistler, British Columbia, Canada
d. New Mexico, U.S.A.

12 What is the name of these hollow tubes that grow from cave ceilings? (Hint: The answer might make you thirsty.)
a. soda straws
b. fire poles
c. hollow bats
d. bean poles

13 What 4,000-year-old treat was found in a cave in New Mexico?
a. a Twinkie
b. popcorn
c. Lucky Charms
d. graham crackers

14 The act of exploring caves is called _____.
a. hiding
b. diving
c. hiking
d. spelunking

CARLSBAD CAVERNS

195

Book 'Em!

This library is anything but quiet—some of the books have come to life! Find and circle the parts of the scene that match the book titles below.

1. Stone Soup
2. Cloudy With a Chance of Meatballs
3. The Hobbit
4. The Polar Express
5. The Lion, the Witch, and the Wardrobe
6. Charlotte's Web
7. Little Women
8. The Cat in the Hat
9. Mr. Popper's Penguins
10. The Chocolate War
11. The Boxcar Children
12. The Little Prince

Just Joking

TONGUE TWISTER!

Say this fast three times:

Seventy-seven silly superstitions.

Q Why did the kitten want to be left alone?

A Because he was in a bad mew-ed.

Where do birds sit at a concert?

In the cheep seats.

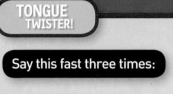

197

HAPPY HOLIDAYS!

1 True or false? The Chinese New Year always takes place on January 1.

2 Which of these trees is most often used as a Christmas tree?

a. fir
b. birch
c. palm
d. weeping willow

3 True or false? Each November, a town in Thailand prepares a special feast for local wild monkeys.

4 About how many **turkeys** are eaten each year on Thanksgiving?

a. 1 million
b. 5 million
c. 20 million
d. 45 million

5 In what country do people celebrate the Day of the Dead?

a. Ireland
b. Japan
c. Mexico
d. Morocco

6 True or false? A shamrock, worn by many people on St. Patrick's Day, is a four-leaf clover.

7 Which vegetable was used to make **Halloween jack-o'-lanterns**, before people started using pumpkins?

a. spinach
b. celery
c. carrots
d. turnips

8 According to legend, what happens if a groundhog sees its shadow on Groundhog Day?

a. there will be six more weeks of winter
b. spring has officially begun
c. there will be no summer
d. winter will last all year

9 In 2011, the most popular Halloween costume for pets was a ____.

a. pumpkin
b. hot dog
c. pirate
d. ghost

10 Rio de Janeiro, Brazil, is famous for its celebration of _____, during which thousands of people in **costumes** parade through the streets.

a. Carnival
b. St. Patrick's Day
c. Christmas
d. Presidents' Day

11 During the Jewish holiday **Hanukkah,** kids receive gifts of chocolate candies that are shaped like what?

a. menorahs
b. flowers
c. stars
d. coins

12 Which holiday—celebrated from December 26 to January 1—means **"first fruits"** in the African language called Swahili?

a. Ramadan
b. Christmas
c. Kwanzaa
d. New Year's Day

13 On **May Day,** children in England welcome spring by dancing around what?

a. a chocolate fountain
b. a piñata
c. a maypole
d. a bean stalk

14 If all of the candy conversation hearts made every year—sold mostly for Valentine's Day—were lined up, how far would they stretch?

a. ten city blocks
b. around the Earth
c. to the moon
d. across the United States twice

Just Joking

Q How do **snowmen** hold things together?

A They use igloo.

Q How did the **lion** greet the **impala**?

A "Pleased to eat you!"

What do you call a pig with three eyes?

A piiig.

Animal Games

These animals can't wait to show off their athletic abilities in the Summer Sports Spectacular. But they ended up at the wrong events. Match each of the ten numbered animals to the correct competition venue.

Pocket PETS

1 Which of the following rodents are considered to be very social?
- **a.** gerbils
- **b.** rats
- **c.** guinea pigs
- **d.** hamsters

2 What should you do if your hamster's teeth turn yellow?
- **a.** Brush them.
- **b.** Change its diet.
- **c.** Take it to a dentist.
- **d.** Nothing. It's normal.

HAMSTER

3 True or false? The smallest gerbil can be as small as about 1.5 inches (3.8 cm) long.

4 Why do you need to give pet rodents wooden chewsticks?
- **a.** to wear down their continually growing teeth
- **b.** because it helps keep them calm
- **c.** so they don't snack too much
- **d.** so they can make the sticks into bedding

5 What is not good to feed a pet mouse?
- **a.** peas
- **b.** apples
- **c.** chocolate
- **d.** food pellets

6 True or false? Chinchillas—rodents from South America—can jump several feet in the air.

CHINCHILLA

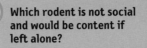

7 Which rodent is not social and would be content if left alone?

a. guinea pig
b. chinchilla
c. gerbil
d. Sonic the Hedgehog

GUINEA PIG

8 Which was one of the first rodents to be domesticated by humans?

a. hamsters
b. rats
c. squirrels
d. guinea pigs

9 Which is a sign of good fortune at the Karni Mata Temple in India, which was built to honor the Hindu rat goddess?

a. having a rat run across your feet
b. eating food nibbled on by a temple rat
c. spying a rare white rat
d. all of the above

10 Which of the following problems can guinea pigs have if they don't get enough vitamin C?

a. bad breath
b. poor eyesight
c. male-pattern baldness
d. scurvy, a condition that causes bleeding and bone problems

11 Which is a healthful diet choice for small rodents?

a. salt
b. cabbage
c. multivitamins
d. your left shoe

12 **True or false?** There are more than 110 species of gerbils in the world.

GERBIL

What in the World?

COLOR YOUR WORLD

These photographs show close-up views of rainbow-colored objects. Unscramble the letters to identify what's in each picture. Bonus: Use the highlighted letters to solve the puzzle below.

TWSASREE

_____

NBRWAOI

_____

ILPNRSKSE

_____

OODCLER ILSNECP

_____

LRBUEALM

_____

HOUSETRTBSHO

_____

RICCELOI

_____

ELOSTW

_____

AESHFRTE

_____

HINT: Leprechaun or not, anyone would be happy to find this under a rainbow.

ANSWER: ___ ___ ___ ___ ___ ___ **G** ___ ___

204

Ski Patrol

Be on the lookout for things that are out of place at this ski resort. Find and circle at least 15 wrong items in this scene.

SKI RENTALS

SKEE SKOOL

Just Joking

Where do bees go on vacation?

Pollenesia.

BRIANNA: Waitress, this soup tastes funny.

WAITRESS: Then why aren't you laughing?

Q Why can't you call the zoo on the phone?

A Because the lion is always busy.

Q

Where do sick fish go?

To the sturgeon.

A

TONGUE TWISTER!

Say this fast three times:

Wayne went to Wales to watch walruses.

Q Why do skunks make terrible waiters?

A Because their service stinks.

207

Eat My Words!

1 Roald Dahl wrote a book about a boy and which kind of giant fruit?
- a. peach
- b. plum
- c. pineapple
- d. pear

2 *Bunnicula* is a story about a bunny that does what?
- a. turns into a bat
- b. bites vegetables and drains them of their juices
- c. grows garlic to fight vampires
- d. lives on a farm in Transylvania

CANDY HEARTS

3 In the nursery rhyme "Little Jack Horner," what was Jack eating?
- a. Christmas pie
- b. Thanksgiving turkey
- c. candy hearts
- d. chocolate eggs

4 In what folktale does a hungry stranger trick a villager into helping him make a delicious meal?
- a. "Yummy Casserole"
- b. "Stone Soup"
- c. "Tricky Pizza"
- d. "Delish Dish"

5 Shel Silverstein's poem "Hungry Mungry" is about a boy who eats which of the following?
- a. a shank of lamb
- b. four chocolate shakes
- c. the universe
- d. all of the above

6 **True or false?** The strange food weather in the book *Cloudy With a Chance of Meatballs* takes place in the village of YumYumville.

7 **True or false?** In the movie *Ratatouille*, Remy the rat creates a delicious vegetable stew.

8 **Which is the name of a book by Judy Blume about a boy who makes a disgusting drink in order to get freckles?**
a. *Freckle Shake*
b. *Freckle Potion*
c. *Freckle Fountain*
d. *Freckle Juice*

9 **Hans Christian Andersen wrote a famous fairy tale about a girl who can feel which food under her mattress?**
a. a soybean
b. a banana
c. a pork chop
d. a pea

10 **In the song "On Top of Spaghetti," what was lost when somebody sneezed?**
a. noodles
b. marshmallows
c. a meatball
d. a sense of humor

11 **True or false?** In the book *The Chronicles of Narnia: The Lion, the Witch and the Wardrobe*, the White Witch gives Edmund a slice of coconut cake at their first meeting.

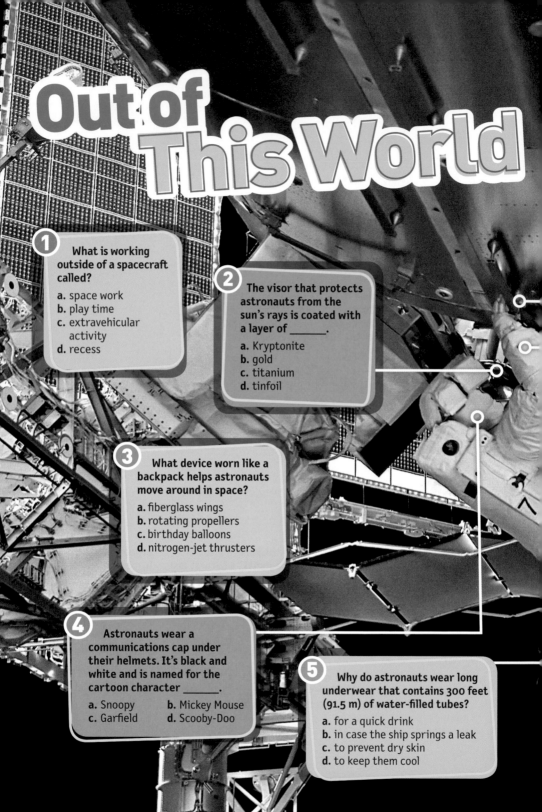

Out of This World

1 What is working outside of a spacecraft called?

a. space work
b. play time
c. extravehicular activity
d. recess

2 The visor that protects astronauts from the sun's rays is coated with a layer of _____.

a. Kryptonite
b. gold
c. titanium
d. tinfoil

3 What device worn like a backpack helps astronauts move around in space?

a. fiberglass wings
b. rotating propellers
c. birthday balloons
d. nitrogen-jet thrusters

4 Astronauts wear a communications cap under their helmets. It's black and white and is named for the cartoon character _____.

a. Snoopy
b. Mickey Mouse
c. Garfield
d. Scooby-Doo

5 Why do astronauts wear long underwear that contains 300 feet (91.5 m) of water-filled tubes?

a. for a quick drink
b. in case the ship springs a leak
c. to prevent dry skin
d. to keep them cool

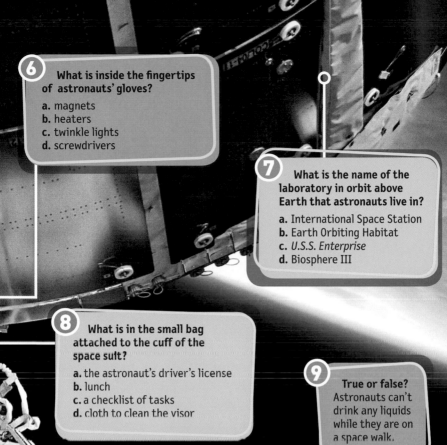

6 What is inside the fingertips of astronauts' gloves?

a. magnets
b. heaters
c. twinkle lights
d. screwdrivers

7 What is the name of the laboratory in orbit above Earth that astronauts live in?

a. International Space Station
b. Earth Orbiting Habitat
c. *U.S.S. Enterprise*
d. Biosphere III

8 What is in the small bag attached to the cuff of the space suit?

a. the astronaut's driver's license
b. lunch
c. a checklist of tasks
d. cloth to clean the visor

9 True or false? Astronauts can't drink any liquids while they are on a space walk.

10 True or false? Astronauts wear adult diapers called Maximum Absorption Garments (MAGs).

AN ASTRONAUT WORKING OUTSIDE OF A SPACECRAFT

11 Which of these is the name of a tool that astronauts use?

a. phaser
b. lightsaber
c. sonic screwdriver
d. pistol grip hand drill

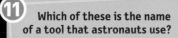

Just Joking

KNOCK, KNOCK.

Who's there?
Sam.
Sam who?
Sam person who knocked before!

Hawaiian monk seals weigh up to 600 pounds (272 kg)—as much as a small horse!

What in the World?

BELOW SEA LEVEL

These photographs show close-up views of underwater creatures. Unscramble the letters to identify each picture. **Bonus:** Use the highlighted letters to solve the puzzle below.

ASE RSAST

_____

CSOUPTO

_____

HAEERSOS

_____

INGALHSEF

_____

ARNTSYIG

_____

EAS GSUL

_____

LBHWIOFS

_____

AES HIURNC

_____

OSTLREB

_____

HINT: It sounds like a vegetable, but it moves along the ocean floor.

ANSWER: _ _ _ _ C _ _ _ M _ _ _ _

DragonVille

1 The Chinese dragon is an **ancient** symbol of what?

a. goodness c. wealth
b. evil d. power

2 In the stories of *My Father's Dragon*, Elmer's baby dragon loves to eat which stinky food?

a. skunk cabbage c. brussels sprouts
b. cat food d. cotton candy

3 What real-life dragon is actually a **300-pound** lizard that was discovered by Europeans 100 years ago?

a. Leafy seadragon
b. Norwegian ridgeback
c. Komodo dragon
d. Charley horse

4 In which popular story is Bastian Bux rescued by the luckdragon?

a. *Beauty and the Beast*
b. *The Neverending Story*
c. *Captain America*
d. *E.T. the Extra-Terrestrial*

5 What popular song for little kids mentions dragons "in a land called **Honah Lee**"?

a. "Ride the Dragon"
b. "Puff, the Magic Dragon"
c. "Little Red Dragon"
d. "Norbert's Song"

6 This 1998 animated movie follows the adventures of a brave girl and her dragon Mushu during China's great Han Dynasty.

a. *Spirited Away* c. *Mulan*
b. *Brave* d. *Eragon*

7 **True or false?**
To frighten enemies, Vikings placed big carved dragon heads on the front of their ships.

8 **In what country do people call themselves "Descendants of the Dragon"?**

a. United States   c. Germany
b. Canada   d. China

9 **This app allows you to raise and care for your own dragons.**

a. DragonVale   c. DragonPark
b. DragonHatch   d. DragonTales

10 **At the end of the 1959 Disney movie *Sleeping Beauty*, who turns into a dragon?**

a. Prince Phillip
b. King Stefan
c. the villain Maleficent
d. Snow White

11 **True or false? The famous line "Never laugh at live dragons, Bilbo you fool!" comes from the classic tale *Charlotte's Web*.**

12 **In a popular book by Christopher Paolini, which teen boy is friends with a dragon named Saphira?**

a. Harry Potter   c. Percy Jackson
b. Eragon   d. Elmer

13 **True or false? Barney is a fierce black dragon who is the star of a children's TV show.**

Just Joking

Red foxes prey on small game, such as rabbits, rodents, and birds.

KNOCK, KNOCK.

Who's there?
Auto.
Auto who?
Auto know, but
I've forgotten.

Q Where do **seals** go to see movies?

A The dive-in.

MOTHER DOG TO PUPPY:

Did you draw pictures all over the walls?

PUPPY:

I can't help it, I'm a labradoodle!

Q What do you call a pig with a sunburn?

A Bacon.

SUN SCREEN 25 SPF

Q

What do you call **a fish** with no **eye?**

A Fsh.

217

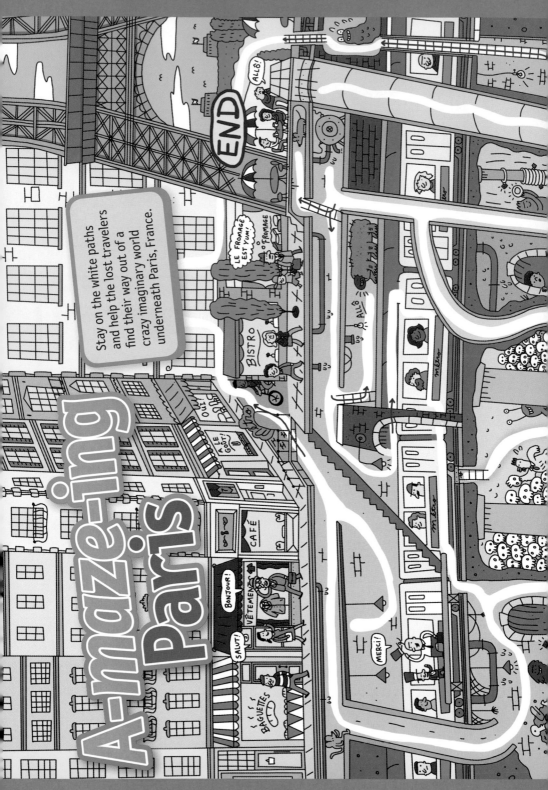

Just Joking

Why did the **spider** cross the road?

To get to the other Web site.

Name That Animal!

2 _____

1 _____

Imagine what a catfish would look like if it were really part cat and part fish. These pictures show how other animals with combination names might appear if they looked exactly like their names. Fill in the correct name of each animal. For example, the first one is part tiger and part shark, so the answer is tiger shark.

3 _____

4 _____

5 _____

221

Valentine Surprise

A rebus is a riddle made up of letters, pictures, and symbols. Can you solve these nine Valentine's Day–themed rebuses?

1 PppOD.

2 🛞 + squirrel -ver **gether gether.**

3 bean - an + mine cart -r.

4 island - land + m + peanuts + **4** + kids - th.

5 U N steak -at R candy **2** eagle↑ -k

6 ice cube -ce **A+** door + arrow sign -turn

7 unicorn -nicorn + rock.

8 lettuce **B** flower↑.

9 Y + oar **M1LLION.**

Rebuses may have been inspired by hieroglyphs, picture-like characters used by the ancient Egyptians to represent words and sounds.

Find the HIDDEN ANIMALS

ANIMALS OFTEN BLEND into their environments for protection. Find the animals listed below in the photographs. Write the letter of the correct photo next to each animal's name.

1. sawblade shrimp ___
2. sand cat ___
3. black bear ___
4. flounder ___
5. white-tailed deer ___
6. white-tailed ptarmigan* ___

Hint: A white-tailed ptarmigan is a type of bird that lives in mountain areas.

A

B

C

D

E

F

Amazing ANTARCTICA

ICE FLOE

1 How much of Antarctica is covered in ice?

a. 25%   c. 83%
b. 49%   d. 98%

SCOTT BASE
SCIENTIFIC CAMP

2 Most people living in Antarctica are scientific researchers. How many people make up the summertime population?

a. 400
b. 4,000
c. 40,000
d. 400,000

3 **True or false?** Antarctica is the windiest place on the planet.

4 Which geographical landmark is located in Antarctica?

a. North Pole
b. South Pole
c. Grand Canyon
d. Mariana Trench

5 The sun never rises in Antarctica during which month of the year?

a. January
b. June
c. March
d. October

6 **True or false?** There are 12 countries on the continent of Antarctica.

ICEBERG OFF THE COAST OF ANTARCTICA

EMPEROR PENGUIN

7 The first successful expedition to the Antarctic took place in the _____.
a. 1540s
b. 1680s
c. 1820s
d. 1930s

8 Which word *best* describes Antarctica?
a. forest
b. desert
c. valley
d. ocean

9 If all of the ice in Antarctica melted, the world's oceans would rise by _____.
a. 49 feet (15 m)
b. 98 feet (30 m)
c. 200 feet (61 m)
d. 394 feet (120 m)

PALM WEEVIL SNOUT BEETLE

10 **True or false?** There are no insects in Antarctica.

11 What does the emperor penguin of Antarctica eat?
a. crabs
b. seals
c. lobster
d. tiny shrimp-like animals called krill

12 What is the average summer temperature in Antarctica?
a. 20°F (–6.7°C)
b. 40°F (4.4°C)
c. 50°F (10°C)
d. 70°F (21.1°C)

225

MONSTER MAZE

Find your way through this haunted cornfield without getting spooked. Then circle ten witch's brooms hidden in the maze.

Just Joking

TONGUE TWISTER!

Say this fast three times:

Peter purchased a pile of perfect presents.

GEORGE GNOME: Are you going ice-skating after school today?

GABBY GNOME: No, the teacher gave me a ton of gnomework.

Why did the **tomato** blush?

Because it saw the salad dressing.

Change of Heart

Love is in the air on this city street, and it has everyone turned around. All of these small scenes are upside-down or sideways. Find each small scene in the big picture.

SIGNS
OF THE TIMES

Seeing isn't always believing. Two of these funny signs are not real. Can you figure out which two are fake?

1

2

HAM
SANDWICH 3 ½

3

SOFT
SHOULDER

4

ON THIS SITE
IN 1897 NOTHING
HAPPENED

6

NO
TURNS
8ᴬᴹ - 7ᴾᴹ
EXCEPT SUNDAY

DONT
LOOK

5

READLYN
"857 friendly people
AND ONE OLD GRUMP"

7

NO
WAY

Aquarium
ANTICS

SEAHORSE

FIDDLER CRAB

1 What is one way that fiddler crabs are helpful in an aquarium?

a. They eat harmful algae.
b. They trim plants with their big claw.
c. They break up fights between other fish.
d. They look tough in there.

2 If a goldfish is given excellent care, how long can it live?

a. up to 1 week
b. 6 months
c. 3 years
d. 20 years or more

3 Which of the following creatures could not live in a freshwater aquarium?

a. minnow
b. rainbow fish
c. horseshoe crab
d. guppy

4 True or false? Angelfish are carnivorous, which means they will eat other fish.

ANGELFISH

5 Do catfish help or harm an aquarium environment?

a. Harm. They sneak up on and scare the other fish.
b. Help. They make the other fish look beautiful.
c. Help. They eat up the food other fish don't eat.
d. Harm. They pick fights with the other fish.

FISH IN AN AQUARIUM

6 Seahorses move mainly by doing what?

a. waiting for the ocean current to move them
b. flapping small fins on their backs
c. curling their tails and using them as pogo sticks
d. calling a taxi

7 Which animal is a trendy aquarium pet in Great Britain?

a. piranha
b. stingray
c. jellyfish
d. dogfish

8 **True or false?** A family in Los Angeles, California, U.S.A., has a fish tank the size of a two-car garage.

9 In China, having a pet fish is good luck because the Chinese word for "fish" sounds like which word?

a. wealth
b. water
c. wisdom
d. wish

GUPPY

10 What is one reason guppies are popular in home aquariums?

a. They bear live young.
b. They lay eggs on the sides of the aquarium.
c. They can do tricks.
d. They like to fight with the other fish.

11 What happens when two male Siamese fighting fish see each other?

a. They dance.
b. They attack each other.
c. They give high fives.
d. They make funny faces.

12 Before glass was invented around 50 B.C., ancient Romans kept their pet fish in what?

a. small tanks made of marble
b. small bowls made of clay
c. large ponds carved from stone
d. large tree trunks

SIAMESE FIGHTING FISH

Just Joking

Green frogs can live for up to ten years!

KNOCK,
KNOCK.

Who's there?
Santa.
Santa who?
Santa card to you last week, did you get it yet?

How do you
catch a
squirrel?

A squirrel can fall up to 100 feet (30 m) without getting hurt! It uses its tail as a parachute.

Climb up a tree and act nuts.

FACE-TO-FACE

These faces aren't staring you down—they're familiar items seen from odd angles. Unscramble the letters to unmask their identities.

NSGPOHPI ABG

ECTSH FO RSDWAER

ALWL KTSCOE

RLEWFO

SIGFHNI ATH

DACBRRDAO OXB

UCP DLI

LMBRAE EACK

POM

Just Joking

Q What do you call a grumpy ex–hockey player?

A No more Mr. Ice Guy.

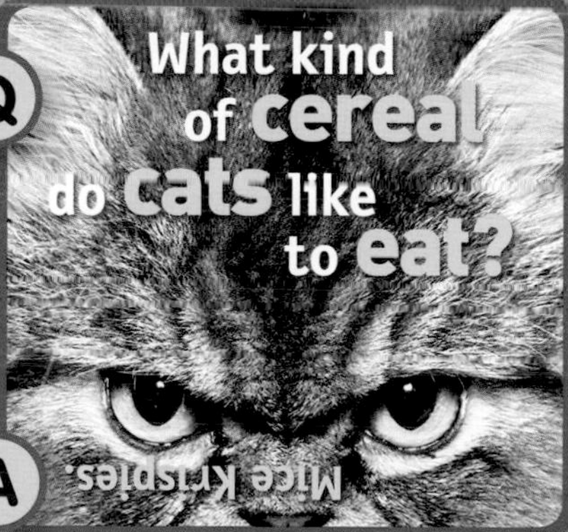

Q What kind of cereal do cats like to eat?

A Mice Krispies.

Q What kind of video game system do witches use?

A A hex-box.

JOE: Why is that knight shouting for a can opener?

RACHEL: He has a bee in his suit.

The Beetles
Gnat King Cole
Black Flag
Sting
Adam Ant

menu

Q What kind of insect listens to music?

A A rockroach.

GOING APE

1 **True or false?** Each gorilla's nose print is unique, like a human fingerprint.

2 The leader of a gorilla group is called a _____.
a. lowlander
b. boss
c. queen gorilla
d. silverback

3 A group of gorillas is called a _____.
a. gaggle
b. troop
c. flock
d. school

4 **True or false?** Gorillas eat mostly meat.

5 About how many mountain gorillas are left on Earth?

a. 90
b. 900
c. 9,000
d. 9 million

6 True or false? Gorillas use sticks to measure the depth of water.

7 Gorillas have a high domed head that ____.

a. supports large muscles for grinding food
b. holds an extra large brain
c. is used to crack open nuts
d. provides room for a mouth full of extra-large teeth

8 Which animal is the gorilla's closest relation?

a. spider monkey
b. brown bear
c. chimpanzee
d. sloth

9 True or false? Gorillas have the same number of teeth as humans.

10 Which of the following is not a real species of gorilla?

a. northern tree
b. eastern lowland
c. western lowland
d. Cross River

11 What body parts do monkeys have that gorillas do not?

a. tails
b. fingers
c. toes
d. knees

12 A captive gorilla named Koko was able to communicate with humans using what?

a. chalk and a blackboard
b. sign language
c. speech
d. toys

13 For how long does a young gorilla share a nest with its mother?

a. 1 to 2 days
b. 3 to 6 weeks
c. 4 to 6 years
d. 12 to 14 years

WESTERN LOWLAND GORILLAS

Noun Town

This city is full of nouns, or people, places, and things. But twelve compound nouns—nouns made up of two or more words, or two words combined to make one word—have been drawn exactly as they're named. Can you guess the compound nouns illustrated in each of the numbered scenes? Here's a hint: The answer to number 1 is "sleeping bag."

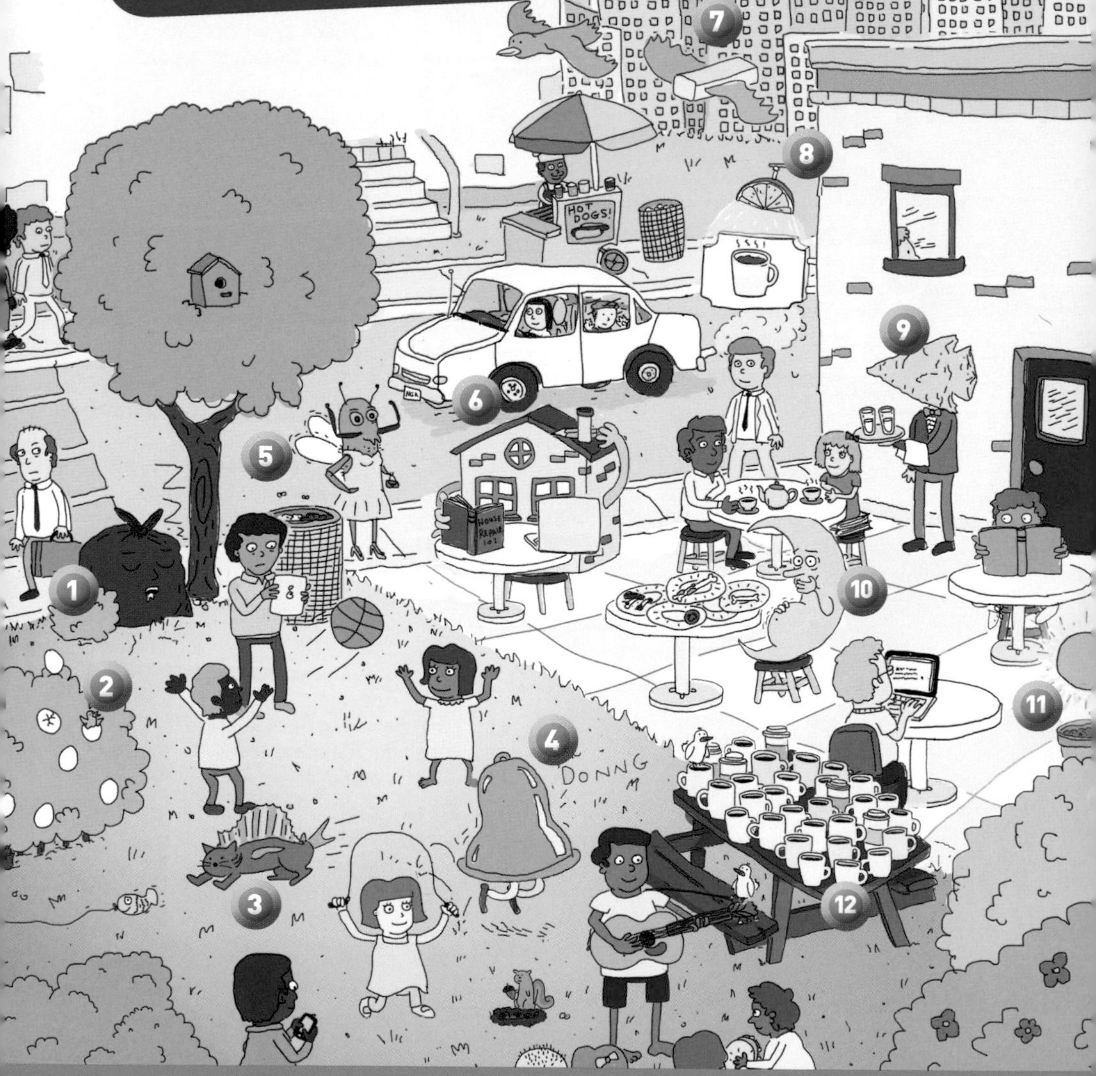

1
2
3
4
5
6
7
8
9
10
11
12
HOT DOGS!
HOUSE REPAIR 101
DONNG

X MARKS THE SPOT

These photos show objects that are either *x*-shaped or have an *x* on them. Unscramble the letters to identify what's in each picture. Bonus: Use the highlighted letters to solve the puzzle below.

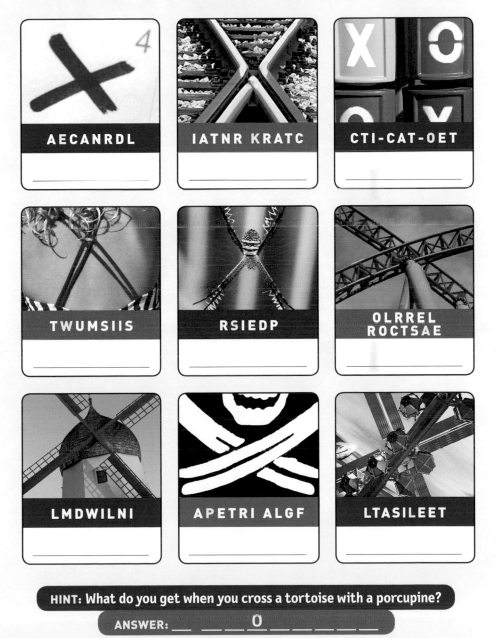

AECANRDL

IATNR KRATC

CTI-CAT-OET

TWUMSIIS

RSIEDP

OLRREL ROCTSAE

LMDWILNI

APETRI ALGF

LTASILEET

HINT: What do you get when you cross a tortoise with a porcupine?

ANSWER: ___ ___ O___ ___ ___ ___ ___

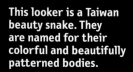

Just Joking

This looker is a Taiwan beauty snake. They are named for their colorful and beautifully patterned bodies.

KNOCK, KNOCK.

Who's there?
Metaphors.
Metaphors who?
Metaphors be with you.

Undersea Stars

This underwater band is jamming onstage, but it looks as if their instruments have disappeared. Or have they? Find the ten instruments listed below hidden in the scene.

1. piano
2. drums
3. flute
4. saxophone
5. triangle
6. violin
7. accordion
8. guitar
9. maracas
10. tambourine

Just Joking

Q Why are cattle so good at math?

$$1 + 1 = ?$$

A Because they use cow-culators.

Q What is the most **terrifying dinosaur?**

A The scare-o-dactyl.

Q How did the pig get to the hospital?

A By ham-bulance.

Q What do birds do on first dates?

A They go on peck-nics.

Q Why did the barber win the race?

A Because he took a short cut.

THE SUNSHINE STATE

These photographs show close-up views of things in Florida. Unscramble the letters to identify what's in each picture. **Bonus:** Use the highlighted letters to solve the puzzle below.

HEBCA ARIHC

_____

NHOCC HLESL

_____

LFPI-OFSLP

_____

LAMP ERTE

_____

LAAILRTGO

_____

SEORGNA

_____

TEKI

_____

VEWA

_____

AIGMNOLF

_____

HINT: What does a manatee use to open a locked door?

ANSWER: ___ ___ ___ ___ ___ ___ ___ D ___ ___ ___ Y

247

A STARRY SHOW

1 **What causes the magnificent light show of the northern lights, also called the aurora borealis?**

a. solar wind streams   c. black holes
b. exploding stars   d. solar eclipses

2 **On what area of Earth's surface can you see the most stars in the sky?**

a. suburban towns   c. large wilderness
b. big cities   areas
                             d. any rooftop

3 **Which planet is Earth's closest neighbor?**

a. Mercury   c. Saturn
b. Venus   d. Neptune

4 **Which is the last stage of the life cycle of most stars?**

a. nebula   c. protostar
b. white dwarf   d. red giant

5 **True or false? The same constellations are always seen in the sky from the same location.**

6 **When gazing at the night sky, what do people often mistake for stars?**

a. helicopters   c. asteroids and
b. planets and   meteors
   satellites   d. the moon

7 **True or false? There is a constellation in the sky that looks like a hunter.**

8 **What causes the shadows and shapes we can see on a full moon?**

a. weather on Earth   c. cheese
b. the man on the   d. craters
   moon

9 **What tool do people use to get the best view of the moon and stars in the sky?**

a. telescope
b. microscope
c. binoculars
d. glasses

10 **True or False? Stars can be seen from Earth in the entire Northern Hemisphere every night of the year.**

11 **The millions of pieces of trash and debris floating around in Earth's atmosphere were caused by _____.**

a. satellite explosions and collisions
b. astronaut garbage
c. launched space vehicles
d. all of the above

12 **In 2004, scientists discovered a star made of _____.**

a. gold
b. diamond
c. dust
d. salt

13 **What object(s) in the sky did sailors use to navigate ships?**

a. clouds
b. the sun
c. the moon
d. constellations

14 **On which planet is a day—the amount of time it takes for a planet to rotate on its axis—longer than 200 Earth days?**

a. Venus
b. Mercury
c. Jupiter
d. Uranus

AURORA BOREALIS

Teeing Off

Find at least 30 items on this miniature golf course that start with the letter *t*.

Just Joking

Q What did the mother broom say to the baby broom?

A Time to go to sweep.

Q Why did the man with one **hand** cross the road?

A To get to the secondhand shop.

Where do smart **hot dogs** end up?

On the honor roll.

MAP MANIA!

Fields of Dreams

① SKI DUBAI

This hot desert country is home to the indoor Ski Dubai resort, which houses a snow-covered hill that is 25 stories high.

a. United Arab Emirates
b. South Africa
c. Mexico
d. Saudi Arabia

② ROMAN COLOSSEUM

In addition to gladiator battles, the Colosseum in Rome, Italy, was flooded on purpose so spectators could watch which type of events?

a. swimming competitions
b. fishing competitions
c. water-ski shows
d. mock naval battles

③ COWBOYS STADIUM

True or False?
The total weight of the giant video board that hangs from the roof of Cowboys Stadium in Dallas, Texas, U.S.A., is 1.2 million pounds (544,310 kg).

NORTH AMERICA

ATLANTIC OCEAN

G E

D

SOUTH AMERICA

PACIFIC OCEAN

252

You'd have to travel the globe to visit all of these sporty venues. Take this quick tour to find out how much you know about these human-made marvels. Then try to match each one to the correct location on the map.

4 WIMBLEDON

Approximately how many tennis balls are used during the 13 days of the Wimbledon tennis tournament in London, England?

a. 500
b. 5,000
c. 50,000
d. 500,000

5 STADIO HERNANDO SILES

Built in the Andes Mountains of La Paz, Bolivia, Stadio Hernando Siles was once banned from hosting World Cup soccer because _____.

a. the stadium's altitude was too high above sea level
b. the stadium's food services were not good enough
c. the playing surface tilted toward one goal
d. the fans were the craziest in the world

ARCTIC OCEAN

EUROPE

ASIA

AFRICA

INDIAN OCEAN

F
A
C
B

6 RUNGRADO MAY DAY STADIUM

With a seating capacity of 150,000, multipurpose Rungrado May Day Stadium in Pyongyang is the world's largest. In which country is this mammoth stadium located?

a. China
b. Japan
c. Australia
d. North Korea

7 CHURCHILL DOWNS

For more than 138 years, Churchill Downs, located in a southeastern state in the U.S.A, has been the home of which famous horse race?

a. the Churchill Challenge
b. the Kentucky Derby
c. the Belmont Stakes
d. the Pinewood Derby

8–14 MATCH EACH SPORTS VENUE
TO THE RED MARKER ON THE MAP THAT SHOWS ITS CORRECT LOCATION.

Going Global

This family is staying home for the winter holidays. But their house is filled with things named after countries (and one continent) from around the world. Find ten of them in this scene. For example, one of the answers is French horn.

Just Joking

ADULT: Can I help you?

KID: How much does it cost to adopt a puppy?

ADULT: Ten dollars apiece.

KID: Ten dollars a piece? I wanted one that was already put together.

TONGUE TWISTER!

Say this fast three times:

Dracula digs dreary, dark dungeons.

Q What happens when a ghost gets lost in the fog?

A He is mist.

Q What do you call two spiders that just got married?

A Newlywebs.

Q What paces back and forth on the ocean floor?

A A nervous wreck.

These eight snapshots were taken
at this theme park.
Find the scene that appears in each snapshot.

257

What in the World?

GO UNDERCOVER!
These photos show close-up views of animals you may recognize. To identify them, unscramble the letters below each picture.

WACAM

MLCA

ODCREIOLC

UJRAGA

FEYTBURTL

REZBA

ERD EPRNPAS

EFRAGIF

OLMHACEEN

Just Joking

Q What is the **nuttiest letter** in the alphabet?

A Cra-Zee.

LEOPARD 1: Can I ask you a question?

LEOPARD 2: Don't put me on the spot!

TONGUE TWISTER!

Say this fast three times:

Real weird rear wheels.

Q Why don't **chickens** make good **house pets?**

A Because they smell fowl.

TONGUE TWISTER!

Say this fast three times:

A glowing gleam glowing green.

Q What do you get if you cross a dog and a telephone?

A A golden receiver.

ANIMAL GROUPIES

1 What is another name for **a litter of kittens?**

a. crew
b. nest
c. kindle
d. nook

2 Which **sea creature** would *not* travel in a school?

a. a shark
b. a dolphin
c. an eel
d. a marlin

3 If you saw hundreds of **grasshoppers** approaching, you'd be correct if you called them a(n) _____.

a. cloud
b. pod
c. army
d. troop

4 A "**coterie**" refers to a group of _____.

a. peacocks
b. prairie dogs
c. butterflies
d. ducks

5 A _____ is another name for a **swarm** of locusts.

a. plague
b. school
c. herd
d. mob

6 True or false? A group of crows can be called a murder.

7 Sometimes, different animals have the same group name. Which **two of these** animal groups would be called an "army"?

a. grasshoppers and elephants
b. caterpillars and frogs
c. grasshoppers and caterpillars
d. caterpillars and elephants

PINK
FLAMINGOS

8 **True or false?**
Walruses live together in groups called prides.

9 **Which of the following words is *not* used to describe a group of giraffes?**
a. herd
b. corps
c. tower
d. height

10 **Which of these is the name for a group of rhinos?**
a. crash
b. knot
c. gaggle
d. stand

11 **Which of the following words can be used to describe a group of oxen?**
a. team
b. yoke
c. drove
d. all of the above

12 **True or false? A group of goldfish is called a troubling.**

13 **As many as 40 meerkats have been known to live together in groups called _____.**
a. mobs
b. herds
c. tribes
d. offices

14 **A leatherback turtle may snack on a smack of ___.**
a. krill
b. plankton
c. jellyfish
d. sharks

15 **A group of flamingos is called a _____.**
a. pink
b. stand
c. leg
d. snooze

Why didn't the **wild pig** get invited to the **party?**

Because he's BOAR-ing!

MARIE: Did you cut the grass today?

GARY: No, I just didn't feel mow-tivated.

Q What kind of fruit should you call if you lock yourself out of the house?

A A key-wi.

Q What do you get if you cross an igloo and a kitten?

A An eski-meow.

TONGUE TWISTER!

Say this fast three times:

Rosie runs rapidly in the rain.

Q What do you call a supercool rodent?

A An awesome possum.

Q Why did the **rapper** carry an **umbrella?**

A Fo' drizzle!

263

Just DESSERTS

1 **True or false?** The ancient Olmec people of Central America are believed to have been the first to make chocolate.

2 Which of these ice-cream flavors has been the most popular in the United States for more than 200 years?
a. chocolate
b. vanilla
c. strawberry
d. Cherry Garcia

3 The world's biggest cupcake weighed 1,315 pounds (596 kg). That's about as heavy as five _____.
a. hippos
b. dump trucks
c. baby elephants
d. cars

4 Girl Scouts have been selling cookies since 1917. What flavor were the first Girl Scout cookies?
a. chocolate chip
b. Thin Mint
c. sugar cookies
d. Samoas

5 **True or false?** In ancient Rome, birthday cakes were usually made only for 50th birthdays.

6 **True or false?** Pumpkin pie was served at the pilgrims' first Thanksgiving.

7 During the 1904 World's Fair in St. Louis, Missouri, U.S.A., a vendor rolled up a waffle-like pastry, creating one of the world's first _____.
a. burritos
b. ice-cream cones
c. funnel cakes
d. wrap sandwiches

8 **True or false?** The name for the graham cracker and chocolate treat called "s'mores" was originally "some mores."

9 What is the name of the dessert made of sponge cake, ice cream, and meringue?
a. snowball
b. baked Alaska
c. ice-cream surprise
d. white wonder

10 Which cartoon character is known for his love of doughnuts?
a. Mickey Mouse   c. SpongeBob Squarepants
b. Homer Simpson   d. Charlie Brown

11 Which of the following was not an original Jell-O flavor when the jiggly treat was introduced in the late 1800s?
a. orange   c. lime
b. strawberry   d. raspberry

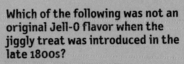

12 The owner of a bed-and-breakfast called the Toll House Inn is believed to have created the first _____ in the 1930s.
a. brownie
b. carrot cake
c. chocolate chip cookie
d. cupcake

13 **True or false?** Gingerbread houses were inspired by the fairy tale *Hansel and Gretel*.

Awesome Autumn

The *Animal Jam* characters are partying in the town square at a fall festival. Find 14 differences between the two scenes below.

WILD GUESS!

Compare these pairs, if you dare.

1 Which is taller?

giraffe ⟷ T. rex

2 Which takes longer?

popping microwave popcorn ⟷ a ride on the world's longest roller coaster

3 Which is heavier?

space shuttle / Leaning Tower of Pisa

4 Which sound travels farther?

a lion's roar ⟷ thunder

5 Which is faster?

the fastest racehorse ⟷ the fastest baseball pitch

6 Which is bigger?

California ⟷ Italy

MAPS NOT TO SCALE

267

Hidden Hike

These hikers are spending St. Patrick's Day exploring Ireland's Cliffs of Moher. But their adventure includes some seriously strange sights. Find and circle at least 15 things that are wrong in the scene.

Jake's science experiment ended with a bang. Now he's late for gym class, and he still has errands to do. Find the route that will get him from the science lab to the stops on his list in order. He can't walk along the same route twice and can't pass the entrances to the teachers' lounge and principal's office.
HINTS: You must pass the entrance to each room on the list. And you must use the stairs to move between floors.

To Do:
1. Return book to library
2. Stop by locker
3. Visit Joe in cafeteria
4. Go to gym class

What do you call a **turtle** wearing a scarf?

Cold.

Box turtles are omnivores. They eat snails, insects, vegetation, and fruit. They have even been known to snack on dead animals!

PURPLE PIZZAZZ

These photos show close-up views of things that are purple. Unscramble the letters to identify what's in each picture. Bonus: Use the highlighted letters to solve the puzzle below.

ISAYD

_____

MULSP

_____

ANRY

_____

TGRETIL

_____

ESA RAST

_____

RSMOMOUH

_____

EILHYJSLF

_____

LOTLAUCCRA

_____

HAMTTYES

_____

HINT: Why did the grape stop in the middle of the road?

ANSWER: __ __ __ __ __ N __ U __ O __ __ I __ __ .

Bowling Freeze-Frame

BFF doesn't stand for only "best friends forever." Can you figure out the three-word phrase that describes each of the numbered scenes in this bowling alley? The first word always begins with **b**, and the second and third words always begin with **f**. For example, the answer to number one is "**B**aboon **f**ries **f**ish."

COAST TO COAST

1 All of the world's oceans cover how much of Earth's surface?

a. 20 percent
b. 55 percent
c. 71 percent
d. 91 percent

2 True or false? Horses first came to Australia by ship with the arrival of Irish and British settlers.

3 What is the name of a dangerous current that can pull swimmers away from a shore?

a. tsunami
b. rip current
c. cross wave
d. neap tide

4 What is a mangrove?

a. a large seashell
b. a bitter fruit shaped like a human head
c. a tree that can grow on sandy seashores
d. a tool used to harvest coconuts

5 What object in space is responsible for high and low tides?

a. moon
b. sun
c. Neptune
d. tidal satellite

6 True or false? Sand dunes are found only in coastal areas.

7 True or false? Sea cliffs are created by waves pounding the lower portion of a rock wall.

8 Which of the following seabirds can swim but not fly?

a. seagull
b. penguin
c. crane
d. puffin

9 If all the world's coastlines were added together, how many miles (km) would they stretch across?

a. 5 miles (8 km)
b. 221,208 miles (356,000 km)
c. 546,000 miles (879,000 km)
d. 10 million miles (16 million km)

10 What is the name of the deepest place in the ocean—located in the Pacific?

a. Enormous Giant Ocean Trench
b. Challenger Deep
c. Deep Pacific Trench Coat
d. Oceanic Southern Trench

11 True or false? There are more grains of sand on Earth than stars in the sky.

12 Coastal grasses help ____.

a. give sand dunes a pretty color
b. pull the sea inland
c. stabilize sand dunes
d. hide sea monsters

13 The most powerful light in a lighthouse today can be seen approximately how far out at sea?

a. 2 feet (.6 m)
b. 10 miles (16 km)
c. 25 miles (40.2 km)
d. all the way across the ocean

COASTAL VIEW OF THE TASMAN SEA BETWEEN AUSTRALIA AND NEW ZEALAND

14 True or false? Canada has a longer coastline than Poland.

15 Seaweed is a type of algae that grows in the water. It has been used for ____.

a. wrapping sushi
b. fertilizing crops
c. polishing shoes
d. all of the above

Just Joking

Bald eagles have excellent eyesight. They can spot a fish while flying up to a mile (1.6 km) overhead!

Why do eagles make great

Because they are very talon-ted.

HOT AND COLD

These photographs show close-up views of hot and cold objects. Unscramble the letters to identify what's in each picture. Bonus: Use the highlighted letters to solve the puzzle below.

CEI MRECA

NSU

YNOSW ERKEC

AALV

REONFZ FITUR

VEOST RUENRB

LECARGI

HIICL PEEPSRP

EIC NKIR

HINT: What do you call icicles hanging from a snowman's face?

ANSWER: __ __ __ __ __ D __ __ __ __ __ D

Game On!

This arcade is packed with fun things to do, but look a little closer. Eleven things beginning with the letter *b* have gone missing. Find the missing items in this scene so the games can go on.

Just Joking

Sea lion

KNOCK, KNOCK.

Who's there?
Avenue.
Avenue who?
Avenue heard enough of these jokes?

Q Why do giraffes have long necks?

A Because they have smelly feet.

TONGUE TWISTER!

Say this fast three times:

Kristin's sister's biscuit mixer.

You've **got** to be joking ...

A sloth was climbing a tree when four snails attacked him. After recovering, he went to tell the police. "Can you describe the snails?" the officer asked. The sloth replied, "Not well. It all happened so fast."

Name That ANIMAL

Many dog and cat breeds are named after different countries. Can you match the international names below with these pets? Write the correct letter next to each animal name below.

1. Russian blue ____
2. English setter ____
3. Siamese cat (Siam is now called Thailand.) ____
4. Afghan hound ____
5. French bulldog ____
6. Persian cat (Persia is now called Iran.) ____
7. English cocker spaniel ____
8. German shepherd ____
9. Irish setter ____
10. Italian greyhound ____

Just Joking

ANNA:
Hey, how did you enjoy the seven-day Sausage Festival?

STEPHEN:
It was the wurst week!

Q

What do you get if a **baker** turns into a **zombie?**

Night of the Living Bread.

A

TONGUE TWISTER!

Say this fast three times:

A tiny tiger thinks tough thoughts.

What do cows and dogs have in common? Q

They both like classical music, Moo-zart and Wag-ner.

A

Q

How do you turn **soup** into **gold?**

Add 24 carrots.

A

Q If chickens wake up when the rooster crows, when do ducks wake up?

At the quack of dawn.

A

281

MAP MANIA!
GOING WILD!

Help these animals find their way home. Match each animal to the continent where it mainly lives in the wild.

① BOBCAT

NORTH AMERICA

SOUTH AMERICA

② GREEN ANACONDA

③ LEOPARD SEAL

④ TOCO TOUCAN

⑤ ADÉLIE PENGUIN

⑥ IBERIAN LYNX

⑦ PANDA

⑧ PLATYPUS

EUROPE

ASIA

AFRICA

OCEANIA

AUSTRALIA

ANTARCTICA

⑨ MOUNTAIN GORILLA

⑩ KANGAROO

⑪ NILE CROCODILE

⑫ BENGAL TIGER

283

Just Joking

Q Why was the archaeologist **upset?**

A His job was in ruins.

Q Why did the gum cross the road?

A Because it was stuck to the chicken's foot.

Q Why are elephants wrinkled?

A Have you ever tried to iron one?

TONGUE TWISTER!

Say this fast three times:

Bob's big black bath brush broke.

CUSTOMER: Do you enjoy being a baker?

BAKER: I sure do— it's a piece of cake!

A female cat is called a queen and a male cat is called a tom.

KNOCK, KNOCK.

Who's there?
Sacha.
Sacha who?
Sacha nice day out today!

GEAR AND GARB

1 What is the largest basketball shoe size in NBA history?

a. 13.5
b. 22
c. 30
d. 16.5

2 High-tech bodysuits for competitive swimmers were banned in 2009 in part because they _____.

a. help swimmers float
b. have fins
c. create too much water turbulence
d. are too colorful

COMPETITIVE SWIMMERS

3 True or False? The equipment a hockey goalie uses in the NHL can weigh as much as 40 pounds (18.1 kg).

4 During the course of the Iditarod sled-dog race, mushers may use around 2,000 of which item?

a. dog-feet booties
b. tissue boxes
c. tubes of lip balm
d. pairs of socks

5 The special skateboards used in the sport of street luge can reach top speeds of _____.

a. 150 mph (241 km/h)
b. 55 mph (88 km/h)
c. 25 mph (40 km/h)
d. 80 mph (129 km/h)

STREET LUGER

6 The proper name for the uniform a wrestler must wear is a _____.

a. tightie-whitey
b. leotard
c. singlet
d. power suit

7 Rackets equipped with string dampeners are supposed to prevent which common tennis injury?

a. tennis toe
b. tennis shoulder
c. tennis elbow
d. tennis wrist

8 Which is the only color horse jockeys cannot wear on their racing silks or uniforms?

a. pea-soup green
b. navy blue
c. beige
d. white

9 True or False? The numbers on the backs of baseball uniforms were originally used to indicate the order in which players batted.

10 A boom, jib, and sloop rig are equipment used in which sport?

a. cycling
b. base jumping
c. boxing
d. sailing

11 How many footballs must the home team provide for an NFL game played outdoors?

a. 15
b. 3
c. 36
d. 1

Just Joking

KNOCK, KNOCK.

Who's there?
Venice.
Venice who?
Venice this door
going to open?

Ducks waddle because their feet are positioned close to their rear ends.

Alive in the

1 How many of Earth's plant and animal species live in the world's rain forests?
a. one-quarter
b. half
c. three-quarters
d. all

2 **True or false?** Orangutans swing from tree to tree in the rain forests of Sumatra and Borneo.

ORANGUTAN

3 How much rain must fall in a forest each year for it to be considered a rain forest?
a. more than 6 inches (15 cm)
b. more than 6 feet (183 cm)
c. more than 60 feet (18 m)
d. more than 600 feet (182 m)

4 The harpy eagle, found in the rain forests of Central and South America, has talons the size of what?
a. a horse's hoof
b. a dog's paw
c. a house cat's paw
d. a grizzly bear's claw

HARPY EAGLE

MACAWS BELONG TO THE PARROT FAMILY.

5 Which of these wild cats prowls the Amazon rain forest?
a. lion
b. jaguar
c. cheetah
d. bobcat

6 Wild parrots, which live in rain forests around the world, can live to be how old?
a. 10 years old
b. 30 years old
c. 60 years old
d. 80 years old

RAIN FOREST

7 True or false? Amazon river dolphins can be pink.

8 Banana plants grow in rain forests in India, Australia, Southeast Asia, and South America. How many bananas can grow in a single bunch?

a. 5
b. 10
c. 50
d. 150

9 Rubber trees are native to the South American rain forests but are now also grown in Southeast Asia and Africa. Which part of the rubber tree is used to make rubber?

a. the bark
b. the sap
c. the leaves
d. the roots

10 Ingredients to make which of the following are found in rain forests?

a. coffee
b. milkshakes
c. grape juice
d. all of the above

11 Which country is home to a third of the world's rain forests?

a. New Zealand
b. Russia
c. Canada
d. Brazil

12 What is the only continent with no rain forests?

a. North America
b. South America
c. Africa
d. Antarctica

A Piece of Cake

Find at least 25 items in this bakery that start with the letter *B*.

Just Joking

Q What has **four eyes** but no **face?**

A Mississippi.

Q How do you make a tissue dance?

A Put a little boogie in it!

Q What do you call a **cheese** that is **not yours?**

A Nacho cheese.

Q What did the water say to the boat?

A Nothing. It just waved.

DJ 1: Oh no! My favorite headphones are broken!

DJ 2: Can't you just get new ones?

DJ 1: No, those were ear-replaceable.

295

The Celebrity SCOOP

1 Which celebrity has won the most Nickelodeon Kids' Choice Awards?

a. Will Smith
b. Taylor Lautner
c. Jack Black
d. Selena Gomez

2 _____ is the voice of Donkey from the *Shrek* series.

a. Cameron Diaz
b. Eddie Murphy
c. Mike Myers
d. Antonio Banderas

3 Johnny Depp has played all of the following characters except ___.

a. Captain Jack Sparrow
b. Willy Wonka
c. Sherlock Holmes
d. The Mad Hatter

4 **True or false?** Cedric Diggory was the first kid to die in the Harry Potter series.

5 Justin Bieber's first hit single was __.

a. "One Time"
b. "Eenie Meenie"
c. "Baby"
d. "Somebody to Love"

6 Which soccer star moved to the United States to play for the Los Angeles Galaxy in 2007?

a. Cristiano Ronaldo
b. David Beckham
c. Thierry Henry
d. Lionel Messi

JUSTIN BIEBER

JOHNNY DEPP

7 Which celebrity did *not* star in a Disney TV show?
- **a.** Selena Gomez
- **b.** Christina Aguilera
- **c.** Rihanna
- **d.** Ashley Tisdale

8 What does Lady Gaga call her fans?
- **a.** Little Gagas
- **b.** Little Monsters
- **c.** Little Giants
- **d.** Little Screamers

9 Who was the first winner on *American Idol*?
- **a.** Kelly Clarkson
- **b.** Carrie Underwood
- **c.** Chris Daughtry
- **d.** Jennifer Hudson

10 Which superstar athlete is known as "The Flying Tomato"?
- **a.** Tony Hawk
- **b.** Shaun White
- **c.** Apolo Anton Ono
- **d.** Michael Phelps

KATY PERRY

11 Which famous singer was the voice of Smurfette in the movie *The Smurfs*?
- **a.** Taylor Swift
- **b.** Beyoncé
- **c.** Katy Perry
- **d.** Miley Cyrus

12 Jaden Smith starred in which remake of a famous movie?
- **a.** *Footloose*
- **b.** *The Karate Kid*
- **c.** *Freaky Friday*
- **d.** *Alice in Wonderland*

Riddle Me This

Answer these riddles! Read the questions below, then find their corresponding punch lines illustrated and marked with yellow dots throughout this museum scene. The first one has been done for you.

1. What kind of shoes do spies wear? *Sneak*-ers
2. What's black and white and pink all over? An embarrassed _ _ _ _ _ _
3. What has bark but no bite? A _ _ _ _
4. What comes down but never goes up? _ _ _ _
5. What's tall when it's young and short when it's old? A _ _ _ _ _ _ _
6. The more you take of these, the more you leave behind. _ _ _ _ _ _ _ _ _ _
7. What has a face and two hands but no arms or legs? A _ _ _ _ _
8. What can honk without a horn? A _ _ _ _ _ _
9. What has a neck but no head? A _ _ _ _ _ _
10. What invention lets you look right through a wall? A _ _ _ _ _ _

Just Joking

Q

What is
taken
before you get it?

A

Your picture.

Q

Why was there thunder and lightning in the lab?

A

Because the scientists were brainstorming.

What do you get when you cross a **cheetah and a french fry?**

Very fast food!

299

PLANT PARTY

1 In the lifetime of a Venus flytrap, how many times can the trap open and close?

a. only once
b. exactly 2 times
c. about 3 or 4
d. more than 50

2 True or false? Hollow baobab trees have been used as a shop, prison, house, storage barn, and even a bus shelter.

3 In order to protect themselves from insects, some trees can _____.

a. turn invisible
b. send chemicals through the air to communicate with each other
c. move to another spot
d. turn into a different kind of tree

4 Which of the following plants shoots its seeds from its pods?

a. witch hazel
b. buttercup
c. flaming arrow shrub
d. daisy

5 What custom is most associated with the mistletoe plant?

a. using the leaves to make firecrackers
b. hiding it for others to find
c. kissing under it
d. using it for a piñata

6 According to legend, which plant keeps werewolves away?

a. marshmallow shrub
b. wolfsbane
c. English ivy
d. yellow wolf away

7 In the Harry Potter series, the Mandrake plant is deadly to anyone who _____.

a. eats its fruit
b. hears its scream
c. says its name aloud
d. smells it

8 True or false? One of the world's most expensive foods is a fungus.

9 Which ice-cream flavor is made from a pod on the flowering orchid?

a. chocolate
c. vanilla
b. tutti-frutti
d. banana

10 True or false? Tomatoes are poisonous when they are green.

11 Which plant has been known to save people stranded in the desert?

a. balloon plant
b. tumbleweed
c. water fountain fern
d. cactus

HOUSEFLY IN
VENUS FLYTRAP

Eyes on the Prize

This archaeologist must find at least ten things in the museum warehouse that have an "eye" sound in their names. Find and circle the items in the scene.

KNOCK, KNOCK.

Who's there?
Ya.
Ya who?
Yahoo!
Ride 'em, cowboy!

Seals use their sensitive whiskers to find food.

Music to Your Ears

1 Which was the title of One Direction's first official song?
a. "I Want It That Way"
b. "What Makes You Beautiful"
c. "Loved You First"
d. "Who Makes Your Dinner"

2 Which country music duo wrote and recorded the hit song "Cruise"?
a. Florida Offensive Line
b. Brooks & Dunn
c. Sugarland
d. Florida Georgia Line

3 Taylor Swift has recorded all the following songs except _____.
a. "We Are Never Ever Getting Back Together"
b. "Our Song"
c. "Beautiful Ears"
d. "I Knew You Were Trouble"

4 True or False? The four hockey-playing members of Big Time Rush come from the state of Minnesota, U.S.A.

5 Adele won an Academy Award for her song "Skyfall" for which international superspy's movie?
a. Austin Powers
b. James Bond
c. Harriet the Spy
d. Agent Cody Banks

6 Which country music superstar has been a coach on the TV show *The Voice* since it first aired?
a. Miranda Lambert
b. Kenny Chesney
c. Blake Shelton
d. Sandy Cheeks

7 Which reality singing competition did singer **Carrie Underwood** win?

a. *The X Factor*
b. *The Biggest Loser*
c. *The Voice*
d. *American Idol*

8 **True or False?** Josh Groban is the lead singer for the band **Maroon 5.**

9 Which is the title of Canadian singer **Carly Rae Jepsen's** song that has been downloaded more than 12 million times?

a. "Love Story"   b. "Call Me Maybe"
c. "Call Me Al"   d. "Tiny Little Bows"

10 By which name are some of **Justin Bieber's** biggest fans known?

a. the Biebs   b. Bieberites
c. Big Biebers   d. Beliebers

12 Who recorded **"Love You Like a Love Song"** and appeared on the TV show *Wizards of Waverly Place*?

a. Selena Gomez   b. Mila Kunis
c. Shakira   d. Emma Roberts

11 Which music star provided the voice for the character Artie in the movie *Shrek the Third*?

a. Justin Timberlake
b. Will Smith
c. Bruno Mars
d. Adam Levine

Just Joking

HA! HA! HA! HA! HA! HA!

KNOCK, KNOCK.

Who's there?
Says.
Says who?
Says me,
that's who!

Young orang-
utans will live
with their
mothers for 11
to 12 years.

GAME ON!

1 **Which character does *not* appear in *Nicktoons MLB*?**

a. Aang
b. Patrick Star
c. Mickey Mouse
d. Sheen Estevez

2 **In the Legend of Zelda video games, the number of lives a player has is usually represented by what?**

a. hearts
b. diamonds
c. swords
d. bananas

3 **In which video game would you find athlete Kobe Bryant?**

a. *Madden NFL 12*
b. *NBA 2K12*
c. *FIFA Soccer12*
d. *Mario & Sonic at the London 2012 Olympics Games*

4 **Which of the following songs can you play in *Guitar Hero World Tour*?**

a. "Baby" by Justin Bieber
b. "You Belong With Me" by Taylor Swift
c. "Who Says" by Selena Gomez and the Scene
d. "Livin' on a Prayer" by Bon Jovi

5 **Which Nintendo video game character is a friend of Mario and Luigi?**

a. Bowser
b. Zelda
c. Princess Peach
d. Donkey Kong

6 **Why are the Angry Birds so angry?**

a. Their eggs have been stolen by green pigs.
b. They haven't gotten much sleep.
c. Their nests have been destroyed by aliens.
d. Their food has been eaten by a pink dinosaur.

7 **Which of the following sports is *not* part of *Wii Sports Resort*?**

a. wakeboarding
b. basketball
c. volleyball
d. Frisbee

8 **True or false?** The object of *Tetris* is to zap as many aliens as possible.

9 Which of the following characters is *not* a video game **villain?**

a. Ganon
b. Donkey Kong
c. Dr. Robotnik
d. Link

10 **Match** each of the following characters to the vintage **video game** it belongs in.

a. alien
b. crocodile
c. frog
d. ghost
e. *Pac-Man*
f. *Space Invaders*
g. *Pitfall*
h. *Frogger*

11 "Sweat," "Duet," and "Simon Says" are all modes of which video game?

a. *Wii Fit*
b. *Just Dance 3*
c. *Rockstar*
d. *American Idol*

12 Which famous **movie series** inspired a Lego video game?

a. Indiana Jones
b. Star Wars
c. Harry Potter
d. all of the above

13 In *Cut the Rope*, players must maneuver **what kind of food** into the mouth of "Om Nom" the monster?

a. a piece of candy
b. a carrot
c. a ham sandwich
d. a cookie

14 Which of these video game consoles came **first?**

a. Nintendo 64
b. PlayStation 2
c. Xbox 360
d. Atari 2600

Just Joking

Harp seal mothers can identify their young by scent alone.

KNOCK, KNOCK.

Who's there?
Albie.
Albie who?
Albie out here if you need me.

WILD DESIGN

These photographs show close-up views of different animal patterns. Unscramble the letters to identify the animal in each picture.

Bonus: Use the highlighted letters to solve the puzzle below.

AGEFRIF

KOECCPA

AMAITDNLA

GBAZR

OIERT

HLSFNOII

SORIOTTE

NYTPOH

RDOLEAP

HINT: Good luck playing hide-and-seek against an animal with this.

ANSWER: _ _ _ _ _ U _ L C A _ U _ _ _ _ _ _

Roman Holiday

These tourists are spending the day at the Colosseum in Rome, Italy. Help the traveler at the top left find his tour group while avoiding the other visitors blocking his path.

START

END

Just Joking

Q Why don't **bicycles** like to get up **early?**

A Because they are two tired.

Q Why did the employee quit his job crushing cans?

A Because it was soda-pressing.

Q What kind of **balls don't bounce?**

A Snowballs.

Q Why did it take the monster ten months to finish a book?

A He wasn't very hungry.

Q Which day of the week do potatoes hate the most?

A Fry-day.

Q What kind of phone calls do choir members make?

A Song distance.

Think Fast!

CLUB-WINGED MANAKIN

1 Zdeno Chara of the Boston Bruins ice hockey team set a National Hockey League record for the fastest slap shot. How fast was it?

a. 4 miles an hour (6 km/h)
b. 55 miles an hour (88 km/h)
c. 108 miles an hour (174 km/h)
d. 697 miles an hour (1,122 km/h)

2 How fast did professional speedster Usain Bolt run the 100-meter dash at the 2012 London Olympics?

a. 2.3 seconds
b. 9.63 seconds
c. 1 minute 4 seconds
d. 10 minutes 17 seconds

BLACK MAMBA

3 If you wanted to outrun the black mamba, the fastest snake in the world, how fast would you need to scoot?

a. only about 5 miles an hour (8 km/h)
b. at least 15 miles an hour (24 km/h)
c. at least 30 miles an hour (48 km/h)
d. at least 60 miles an hour (97 km/h)

4 Which car can reach speeds of 267 miles an hour (430 km/h)?

 a. Chevrolet Corvette

 b. Alfa Romeo

 c. Volkswagen Beetle

 d. Bugatti Veyron Super Sport

5 China's CRH380A is the fastest way to travel on land legally. What is the CRH380A?

a. a group of cars chained together
b. a tour bus for a rock-and-roll band
c. a train
d. a horse that drank a lot of coffee

6 The male club-winged manakin can flap its wings the fastest of any bird. Why this need for speed?

a. to attract a mate
b. to fly into space
c. to fan away pests
d. to make humming-birds feel like losers

7 Which animal can run more than 40 miles an hour (64 km/h), making it the world's fastest running bird?

a. an ostrich
b. a penguin
c. a roadrunner
d. a kiwi

8 True or false? The fastest any human has ever traveled is 24,791 miles an hour (39,897 km/h).

9 The fastest piloted airplane can travel more than 2,000 miles an hour (3,218 km/h). What is its name?

a. the Blackberry
b. the Black Panther
c. the Blackbird
d. the Holy Cow That's Fast!

GENTOO PENGUIN

10 Which bird of prey can dive at speeds that are faster than the average race car can drive?

a. a chicken
b. a peregrine falcon
c. a turkey vulture
d. a duck

11 Where is the world's fastest roller coaster?

a. Six Flags, Jackson, New Jersey, U.S.A.
b. Cedar Point, Sandusky, Ohio, U.S.A.
c. Fuji-Q Highland, Yamanashi, Japan
d. Ferrari World, Abu Dhabi, U.A.E.

ROLLER COASTER

Birthday Bash!

These two birthday parties may seem the same at first glance, but there are actually 20 differences between the scenes. Find and circle the differences.

HAPPY BIRTHDAY!

Happy Birthday!

HAPPY BIRTH

Just Joking

The Arabian stallion is one of the world's oldest breeds of riding horse.

KNOCK, KNOCK.

Who's there?
Amos.
Amos who?
A mosquito bit me.

ANIMAL JAM®

It's a Jungle Out There!

The characters from *National Geographic Animal Jam* created a party game to help *NG Kids* magazine celebrate its 35th birthday. They've hidden 35 items (including themselves) throughout the scene. Can you find them all before the evil phantom does?

1. coins
2. scroll
3. magnifying glass
4. Graham the monkey
5. green gem
6. Cosmo the koala
7. green sea star
8. ladybug
9. butterfly
10. telescope
11. book
12. map
13. owl
14. cactus
15. blue gem
16. shovel
17. banana
18. red gem
19. hat
20. fire
21. watermelon
22. sand castle
23. beach ball
24. bird
25. surfboard
26. mask
27. spears
28. butterfly net
29. wind chime
30. Peck the rabbit
31. evil phantom
32. Greely the wolf
33. bottles with herbs
34. Sir Gilbert the tiger
35. Liza the panda

Fashion Forward

1 If you were wearing a "union suit" in the 1800s, which would you have on?
- **a.** matching shirt and pants
- **b.** a Civil War costume
- **c.** long underwear
- **d.** snorkel and fins

2 Which of the following is the oldest type of clothing item?
- **a.** toga
- **b.** hat
- **c.** skirt
- **d.** loincloth

3 Which did Levi Strauss get a patent to make in 1873?
- **a.** work boots
- **b.** tutus
- **c.** flannel shirts
- **d.** denim jeans

4 If you lived in the 1920s and saw a "flapper," what would you be looking at?
- **a.** a chicken suit
- **b.** a woman who dressed in a certain style
- **c.** an early version of a helicopter
- **d.** a pilot's outfit

5 A kimono is a fancy dress, often made from silk. Where was it first used?
- **a.** Japan
- **b.** Mexico
- **c.** Transylvania
- **d.** Egypt

6 **True or false?** Two thousand years ago, Roman citizens were not allowed to wear togas to gladiator combat games.

KIMONO

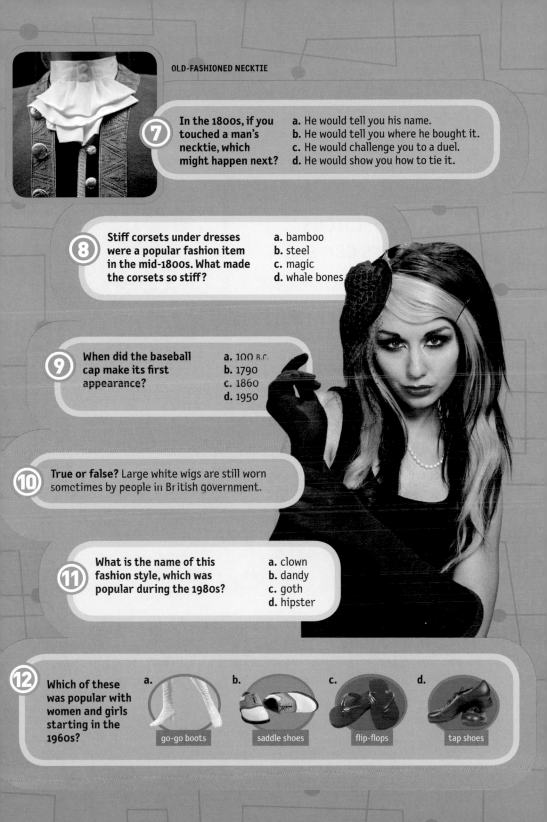

OLD-FASHIONED NECKTIE

7 In the 1800s, if you touched a man's necktie, which might happen next?

a. He would tell you his name.
b. He would tell you where he bought it.
c. He would challenge you to a duel.
d. He would show you how to tie it.

8 Stiff corsets under dresses were a popular fashion item in the mid-1800s. What made the corsets so stiff?

a. bamboo
b. steel
c. magic
d. whale bones

9 When did the baseball cap make its first appearance?

a. 100 B.C.
b. 1790
c. 1860
d. 1950

10 True or false? Large white wigs are still worn sometimes by people in British government.

11 What is the name of this fashion style, which was popular during the 1980s?

a. clown
b. dandy
c. goth
d. hipster

12 Which of these was popular with women and girls starting in the 1960s?

a. go-go boots
b. saddle shoes
c. flip-flops
d. tap shoes

Just Joking

JIM: Which circus performers can see in the dark?

NANCY: The acro-bats.

Q

What is the **center** of gravity?

A The letter V.

Q Who are a hamburger's favorite people?

A Vegetarians.

Q What looks like half a tomato?

A The other half.

Q Why did the **belt** go to jail?

A Because it held up a pair of pants.

We Gave It a Swirl

Use the clues below to figure out which animals appear in these swirled pictures.

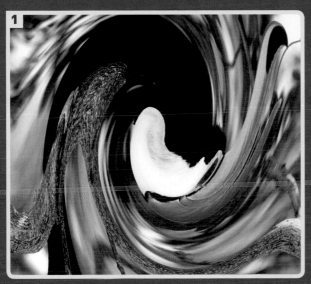

1

HINT: A bright beak makes this South American native stand out in the trees.

2

HINT: It wears a fur coat even during summer.

3

HINT: Instead of legs, this underwater creature uses five arms to get around.

4

HINT: Its unique pattern actually helps this animal blend in at a family reunion.

5

HINT: If someone tells you this marine mammal loves to swim, they're not "lion."

Color Café

Some items in this scene have mysteriously changed color. Find at least 12 things that are the wrong color.

SIGNS
OF THE TIMES

Seeing isn't always believing. Two of these funny signs are not real. Can you figure out which two are fake?

INCREDIBLE INVENTIONS

1 Which classic **amusement park ride** was modeled after a bicycle wheel?

a. bumper car
b. Ferris wheel
c. roller coaster
d. tea cup ride

2 **True** or **false?** The Popsicle was invented by an 11-year-old boy.

3 True or false? A man invented a **ringtone** that can be heard only by **young people.**

4 Most experts believe **fireworks** were invented in what country?

a. Greece
b. Egypt
c. Canada
d. China

5 Before modern **toothbrushes were invented** in 1938, what were toothbrush bristles made of?

a. horsehair
b. porcupine quills
c. cat whiskers
d. hog hair

6 In 1782, Joseph Michel Montgolfier filled a silk bag with **hot air.** What did he invent?

a. a birthday balloon
b. an air mattress
c. a hot-air balloon
d. water wings

7 The **first cell phone** weighed two pounds (0.9 kg), the weight of _____ iPhones.

a. three
b. four
c. five
d. six

8 In the movie *Hugo*, what invention does **Hugo** try to repair?

a. a camera
b. an automaton
c. a radio
d. a video game console

9 In the movie *The Nutty Professor* Sherman Klump invents a special potion. What does it do?

a. makes his hair fall out
b. makes him skinny
c. makes him grow
d. makes him fly

10 Before the invention of **penicillin**, what was often used to clean infected wounds?

a. soup
b. worms
c. aspirin
d. maggots

11 The "Snurfer"— a flat board that people used to "surf" on snow—led to what invention?

a. surfboard
b. skateboard
c. snowboard
d. kiteboard

12 **TOPIO** is a humanoid robot that is designed to ___.

a. clean your room
b. play Ping-Pong
c. rescue people
d. explore planets

13 True or false? The fortune cookie was invented in China.

ANSWERS

It's a Jungle Out There! page 6

To Infinity ... and Beyond! pages 8–9

1. **a**
2. **b**
3. **d**
4. **d**
5. **c**
6. **c**
7. **Gross but true.** (The urine is passed through a recycling system on the station.)
8. **c**
9. **c**
10. **d**
11. **a**
12. **b**

Bizarre Buffet, page 11

Survival Guide, pages 12–13

1. **a**
2. **d**
3. **True.** A person can survive in the wilderness by eating a variety of insects, fish, birds, and small mammals. Don't try this at home—or anywhere!
4. **b**
5. **False.** Rubbing frostbitten skin will damage the tissue further. Get your toes into warm—not hot—water.
6. **a**
7. **c**
8. **False.** The inner bark of pine trees contains sugars, starches, and calories. People have scraped and cooked it so that it can be digested.
9. **a**
10. **True.** Small fish such as minnows can be scooped up with a T-shirt. Larger fish can be speared with a stick.
11. **a**
12. **b**
13. **a**
14. **a**

Animal Jam, Treasure Hunt, page 14

Monster Match, pages 16–17

What in the World? Heads or Tails? page 19

Top row: **cat whiskers, camel hump, moose antler**
Middle row: **snake tongue, whale tail, gecko foot**
Bottom row: **octopus tentacles, blue-footed booby foot, rooster comb**
Bonus: **centipede**

Pick a Number ... pages 20–21

1. **a**
2. **c**
3. **b**
4. **True.** Also, when you write out the numerals 0–10, the letter "e" occurs ten times.
5. **a**
6. **False.** It equals 100.
7. **a**
8. **a**
9. **True.** So the total number of dots is 21.
10. **c**
11. **d**

Signs of the Times, page 22

Signs **5** and **7** are fake.

Double Take, page 24

Go Fish! page 25

Earthly Extremes, pages 26–27

1. **b**
2. **d**
3. **d**
4. **True.** The Challenger Deep, located in the Mariana Trench in the Pacific Ocean, is almost seven miles (11 km) deep. If Mount Everest were placed inside, there would still be more than 6,000 feet of water above it.

5. **b**
6. **b**
7. **d**
8. **d**
9. **d**
10. **True.** The high salt levels in the Dead Sea keep people afloat.
11. **d**

Color Coded, page 29

Funny Money, page 30

1. **Too high.** Real price: $2,614
2. **Too high.** Real price: $1.56 million
3. **Too low.** The Mona Lisa is priceless.
4. **Too high.** Real price: $2.2 million
5. **Too low.** Real price: $15.15 (average)
6. **Correct.**

What in the World? Seeing Spots! page 31

Top row: **twister, feather, gecko**
Middle row: **ladybug, Dalmatian, domino**
Bottom row: **fish, candy buttons, mushroom**

Map Mania! Wonders of the World, pages 32–33

1. **a**
2. **c**
3. **c**
4. **d**
5. **c**
6. **True.** Inca workers likely used ropes and levers to move heavy stones up the towering mountain.
7. **b**
8. Taj Mahal—**F-Agra, India**
9. Colosseum—**D-Rome, Italy**
10. Christ the Redeemer Statue—**C-Rio de Janeiro, Brazil**
11. Chichén Itzá—**A-Yucatán, Mexico**
12. Great Wall—**G-China**
13. Machu Picchu—**B-near Cusco, Peru**
14. Petra—**E-southwest Jordan**

Bark Park, page 35

329

City Gone Wild!
page 36

Double Take,
page 42

Make a Splash!
page 47

1. pie in the sky
2. raining cats and dogs
3. out on a limb
4. pulling your leg
5. water under the bridge
6. get your ducks in a row
7. fly on the wall
8. bite off more than you can chew
9. ants in your pants
10. cat's got your tongue

Toy Stories,
pages 44–45

1. c
2. **True.** HexBugs react to sounds, light, and pressure.
3. c
4. d
5. c
6. d
7. b
8. d
9. c
10. **True.** Astronauts on the Apollo 8 mission used Silly Putty to hold down floating tools.
11. **False.** They were called Matchbox cars because they fit inside a matchbox.
12. b

Signs of the Times,
page 48

Signs **2** and **6** are fake.

Mythical Mix-Up,
page 49

1. The dragon's tail is with the leprechaun
2. genie's lamp: Bigfoot
3. mermaid's fins: fairy
4. wizard's wand: yeti
5. Cyclops's eye: unicorn
6. unicorn's horn: genie
7. yeti's hair: dragon
8. Bigfoot's foot: mermaid
9. leprechaun's pot of gold: wizard
10. fairy's wings: Cyclops

What in the World? Game On!
page 37

Top row: **checkers, Monopoly, chess**
Middle row: **Clue, Scrabble, Sorry!**
Bottom row: **Operation, Connect Four, Mouse Trap**
Bonus: **a cool beard**

What in the World? Dynamic Duos,
page 40

Top row: **fuzzy dice, socks, earrings**
Middle row: **scissors, twins, playing cards**
Bottom row: **jeans, binoculars, in-line skates**
Bonus: **Batman and Robin**

Also Known As,
page 41

1. ape knits alphabet
2. astronomer knights athlete
3. astronaut kicks airplane
4. artist kisses aunt
5. alligator kayaks alley
6. armadillo kings actor
7. alien knots apron

What in the World? Fun in the Sun,
page 46

Top row: **wave, swim trunks, chair**
Middle row: **seashells, crab, seagull**
Bottom row: **sailboat, sunglasses, flip-flop**
Bonus: **hang ten**

What in the World? Wild Range,
page 52

Top row: **elephant, gibbon, vine snake**
Middle row: **crocodile, red lory, otter**
Bottom row: **sun bear, rhinoceros, tarsier**
Bonus: **They eat whatever bugs them.**

ANSWERS

Find the Hidden Animals, page 53

1. D
2. E
3. F
4. C
5. A
6. B

Bugging Out, pages 54–55

1. a
2. **True.** Because many people have serious allergies to bee stings, honeybees kill dozens of people a year in the United States while only a handful of people die from snakebites.
3. d
4. c
5. **True.** The diseases mosquitos carry kill 2–3 million people each year.
6. b
7. b
8. b
9. d
10. b
11. **False.** The brown bat can eat only about 2,000–6,000 insects in a single night.
12. d
13. d

Obstacle Course Chaos, page 56

Panda-monium, page 57

Shark Bites, pages 58–59

1. b.
2. c
3. **True.** The great white shark's skin is made of tiny, toothlike structures that make it feel rough.
4. b
5. d
6. c
7. d
8. a
9. **True.** Great white sharks can weigh more than 5,000 pounds (2,268 kg).
10. d
11. c
12. b
13. b
14. d
15. c

What in the World? Hello, Yellow, page 60

Top row: **roses, ducklings, banana**
Middle row: **mustard, frog, raisins**
Bottom row: **shopping carts, rain boots, butterflies**

The Wide World of Sports, pages 62–63

1. d
2. **True.** Blue represents Europe, yellow represents Asia, black represents Africa, green represents Oceania, and red represents the Americas.
3. d
4. **True.** Players use sharp objects in their kites to cut their opponents' kite strings.
5. c
6. a
7. c
8. a
9. c
10. b
11. d
12. **True.** In Malaysia, "foot tennis" involves passing a ball across a net using the feet, knees, and thighs.

What in the World? Best of the Northwest, page 64

Top row: **redwood trees, Space Needle, sea otter**

Middle row: **red rock crab, totem pole, kelp forest**

Bottom row: **Mount Hood, orca, seaplane**

Bonus: **He needed to tuna fish.**

Famous Pairs, pages 66–67

1. **c**
2. **c**
3. **d**
4. **b**
5. **True.** Pinky and the Brain are laboratory mice who live in Acme Labs.
6. **c**
7. **d**
8. **False.** Mario and Luigi are brothers who work as plumbers.
9. **a**
10. **c**
11. **a**
12. **a**

Up, Up, and Away, page 68

Trivia Tech Zone, pages 70–71

1. **c**
2. **d**
3. **c**
4. **c**
5. **a**
6. **a**
7. **True.** About 30,000 visitors viewed videos on YouTube each day when it launched in 2005.
8. **b**
9. **d**
10. **True.** The bid reached $3,000 before eBay removed it due to policy violation. Apparently countries are not for sale!
11. **a**
12. **d**

Spellbound, page 74

1. **baboon**
2. **eel**
3. **snake**
4. **duck**
5. **owl**
6. **kitten**
7. **otter**
8. **parrot**
9. **crickets**
10. **spider**

What in the World? Rain Forest Roundup, page 76

Top row: **frog, bat, sloth**

Middle row: **jaguar, viper, piranha**

Bottom row: **grasshopper, tapir, toucan**

Bonus: **a howler monkey business**

The Amazing Human Machine, pages 78–79

1. **c**
2. **c**
3. **b**
4. **a**
5. **a**
6. **a**
7. **c**
8. **b**
9. **False.** Tiny eight-legged mites are always living in your eyelashes.
10. **c**
11. **a**
12. **b**

Trading Places, pages 80–81

1. **bullfrog**
2. **giraffe**
3. **camel**
4. **clown fish**
5. **emperor penguin**
6. **orangutan**
7. **brown bear**

Mystery Maize, page 82–83

Funniest Fads of All Time, pages 84–85

1. a
2. **True.** Swallowing goldfish caught on in 1939. The world-record holder swallowed 300 goldfish in one sitting.
3. c
4. d
5. **True.** The earliest examples of tie-dye date back to A.D. 500 in an area that is present-day Peru.
6. b
7. a
8. a-h, b-e, c-g, d-f
9. b
10. c
11. b
12. a
13. a

What in the World? Spotted in Nature, page 86

Top row: **fish, bird eggs, cheetah**
Middle row: **fawn, frog, mushroom**
Bottom row: **beetle, flower, squid**
Bonus: **Dalmatian**

Pirates' Cove, pages 88–89

1. **False.** Pirates attacked other ships to steal the treasures and weapons on board, and the ship itself.
2. **False.** While most pirates were men, there were a few female outlaws on the high seas. Two of the most famous female pirates were Anne Bonny and Mary Read.
3. b
4. a
5. **False.** Most pirates spent the treasure they stole. The only pirate known to have buried treasure is William Kidd.

6. c
7. d
8. a
9. **False.** The writers of the movies claim Jack Sparrow was inspired by Bugs Bunny and comedian Groucho Marx.
10. c
11. a
12. d
13. **False.** Pirates believed that earrings helped prevent seasickness by pressing on the earlobes.
14. d
15. **True.** Pet parrots were common among pirates who spent time around Central America, where parrots are found in the wild.

Mousetrap, page 91

Take the Plunge, page 92

What in the World? Into Darkness, page 93

Top row: **ants, roots, millipede**
Middle row: **mole, beetle, tarantula**
Bottom row: **larva, fossil, cicada**
Bonus: **monster mashed potatoes**

Mark Your Calendar, pages 94–95

1. c
2. a
3. d
4. a
5. **True.** Many cultures hold this celebration to welcome spring.
6. b
7. b
8. **False.** A day on Mars is about 40 minutes longer than a day on Earth.
9. c
10. **True.** In France, the one who is being pranked is called *poisson d'avril*, or "April fish." The term may have originated from a reference to a young fish that is easily caught.
11. b
12. a
13. c

Find the Hidden Animals, page 96

1. C
2. D
3. B
4. F
5. A
6. E

What in the World? I See London, page 97

Top row: **crown, British flag, Tower Bridge**

Middle row: **double-decker bus, London Eye, guard**

Bottom row: **Buckingham Palace, fish and chips, Piccadilly Circus**

Bonus: **knight vision**

Mind Your Manners, pages 98–99

1. **a**
2. **a**
3. **True.** It resembles incense burning, symbolizing offering food for the dead.
4. **b**
5. **d**
6. **b**
7. **d**
8. **c**
9. **False.** Slurping is considered an acceptable and enjoyable way to eat soup in Japan.
10. **b**
11. **d**

Powers of Nature, pages 100–101

1. **a**
2. **b**
3. **c**
4. **b**
5. **b**
6. **a**
7. **c**
8. **b**
9. **b**
10. **False.** The storm lasted for four days.
11. **c**

What in the World? Think Pink, page 103

Top row: **flamingos, hot-air balloon, dougnut**

Middle row: **worms, tongue, feather**

Bottom row: **katydid, crystal, seahorse**

Bonus: **bubble gum**

Movie Greats, pages 104–105

1. **d**
2. **a**
3. **c**
4. **c**
5. **b**
6. **b**
7. **b**
8. **False.** Nickelodeon is named after movie theaters from the early 1900s called Nickelodeons, where people paid a nickel to watch a series of short movies.
9. **d**
10. **a**
11. **b**
12. **c**
13. **c**

Perfect Match, pages 106–107

We Gave It a Swirl, page 108

1. **clown fish**
2. **cheetah**
3. **duckling**
4. **polar bear**
5. **caterpillar**

Save Our Ship! page 109

1. **sailor operates saw**
2. **shopkeeper organizes sunscreen**
3. **seagulls overload sailboat**
4. **swimmer offers sandwich**
5. **sheepdog obeys surfer**
6. **soldier opens safe**
7. **snorkeler orders sundae**

Ready, Set, Eat! page 111

Doggone Fun! pages 112–113

1. **b**
2. **False.** Dalmatian puppies are born with no spots at all.
3. **True.** From tiny teacup poodles to huge Great Danes, most adult dogs have about 320 bones and 42 teeth.
4. **a**
5. **c**
6. **c**
7. **d**
8. **c**
9. **c**
10. **b**
11. **d**
12. **c**

ANSWERS

Dinner Party in the U.S.A., page 114

Ancient Egypt, pages 116–117

1. b
2. c
3. d
4. d
5. **True.** Wealthy Egyptians mummified pets as a sign of respect, including cats, dogs, birds, and monkeys.
6. a
7. a
8. **True.** Rulers in ancient Egypt weren't allowed to show their hair. Instead they wore headdresses called nemes.
9. d
10. b
11. b
12. **True.** Both men and women wore makeup in ancient Egypt, originally as protection from the sun.
13. b
14. b
15. **False.** Some Egyptian mummies have been found buried in the sand.

What in the World? The Hole Thing, page 118

Top row: **doughnut, Swiss cheese, guitar**
Middle row: **rabbit hole, inner tube, keyhole**
Bottom row: **cereal, honeycomb, golf hole**
Bonus: **a hole in one**

Animal Speak, pages 120–121

1. a
2. d
3. a
4. d
5. d
6. **True.** Some piranhas make barking, croaking, and clicking noises.
7. d
8. a
9. **False.** Snakes stick out their tongues to smell. To communicate, they sometimes use body movements and scents.
10. a
11. **True.** A zebra's stripes are as unique as a human's fingerprints.
12. c

Map Mania! You Saw It Here First, pages 122–123

1. **Kites: China**
2. **Returning boomerangs: Australia**
3. **Electric guitars: United States**
4. **Breath Mints: Egypt**
5. **Pizza: Italy**
6. **Flushing toilets: United Kingdom**
7. **Velcro: Switzerland**
8. **Yo-yos: Greece**
9. **Hot-air balloons: France**
10. **Space satellites: Russia/U.S.S.R.**
11. **Chess: India**

Safari Race, page 125

Traveling Circus, pages 126–127

1. c
2. a
3. b
4. d
5. d
6. b
7. d
8. **False.** They always step out on their right foot for good luck.
9. c
10. **True.** Bozo the Clown has been played by more than 100 actors over the years.
11. a
12. b
13. a
14. d

What in the World? Going Global, page 128

Top row: **Statue of Liberty, Stonehenge, Golden Gate Bridge**
Middle row: **Great Wall of China, Big Ben, Eiffel Tower**
Bottom row: **Machu Picchu, Taj Mahal, Sphinx**
Bonus: **the Hollywood Sign**

Slithery Slimy Search!
page 130

Dive In,
page 131

Treasure Hunt,
pages 132–133

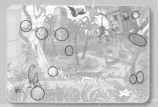

Be Polite Around the Globe,
pages 134–135

1. a
2. c
3. a
4. b
5. b

6. c
7. c
8. a
9. c
10. **True.** It's considered rude because your host will think that you did not get enough food.
11. **True.** A light handshake is fine, though most people—even in areas of business—kiss each other once on each cheek instead.
12. c
13. d
14. c

Undersea Skiing,
page 138

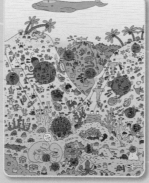

Wonders of Nature,
pages 140–141

1. b
2. c
3. a
4. a
5. d
6. **True.** The eel can produce an electric shock with about as much energy (500 watts) as five lightbulbs.
7. c
8. **True.** Some seals living in the Arctic can hold their breath for an hour or more under the ice.
9. c
10. d
11. a
12. d

What in the World? Heart-to-Heart,
page 142

Top row: **cloud, rope, leaf**
Middle row: **flower, islands, potato**
Bottom row: **computer mouse, ravioli, door handle**
Bonus: **You eat it.**

Splashdown,
pages 144–145

Body Parts,
pages 146–147

1. a
2. d
3. b
4. b
5. c
6. **True.** The cerebellum, part of your brain, warns the rest of your brain that you are about to tickle yourself so the sensations are ignored.
7. a
8. c
9. a
10. a
11. a
12. b
13. d

Get Spooked!
page 148

Greek Mythology, pages 152–153

1. d
2. a
3. a
4. a
5. b
6. **False.** Everything King Midas touched turned to gold.
7. b
8. b
9. c
10. c
11. **False.** Aphrodite was the goddess of love. The queen of the gods was Hera.
12. d

Animal Jam, Scout It Out, page 155

U.S. Presidents, pages 156–157

1. b
2. c
3. a-h, b-e, c-f, d-g
4. c
5. **False.** Legend has it that George Washington had wooden teeth, but he actually wore dentures made from gold, ivory, lead, and human and animal teeth.
6. b
7. d
8. a-f, b-e, c-h, d-g
9. b
10. **True.** Other African Americans have run for the office, but Obama is the first to have been elected.
11. b
12. b
13. b
14. a
15. c

What in the World? Change Your Stripes, page 158

Top row: **tiger, octopus, butterfly**
Middle row: **jellyfish, snail, chameleon**
Bottom row: **turtle, hermit crab, zebras**

Map Mania! Still Standing, pages 160–161

1. a
2. **True.** The Eiffel Tower was built for the 1889 World's Fair.
3. b
4. **True.** The tower started leaning as workers built the third story.

5. c
6. b
7. b
8. Big Ben—London, England
9. Eiffel Tower—Paris, France
10. The Sphinx—Giza, Egypt
11. Leaning Tower of Pisa—Pisa, Italy
12. The Kremlin—Moscow, Russia
13. The Forbidden City—Beijing, China
14. Blarney Castle—Blarney, Ireland

Map Mania! Great Adventure, pages 164–165

1. a
2. d
3. d
4. c
5. d
6. b
7. b
8. Zambezi River—F
9. Alaska, U.S.A.—C
10. Antarctica—G
11. Guadalupe Island, Mexico—E
12. Mount Everest—B
13. Australia—D
14. Galápagos Islands—A

What in the World? Gold Standard, page 166

Top row: **gold bars, trophy, keys**
Middle row: **watch, statue, gold nuggets**
Bottom row: **crown, coin, French horn**
Bonus: **Olympic gold medal**

ANSWERS

Animal Jam, Twinkle Toes, page 167

1. panda
2. monkey
3. bunny
4. koala
5. avatar
6. tiger
7. fox

And Now for My Next Trick ... pages 168–169

1. b
2. a
3. **True.** The stones help grind the meat they have eaten.
4. c
5. b
6. c
7. b
8. **True.** The creatures use the ooze to stun their enemies while they escape.
9. b
10. d
11. c
12. **False.** Spiders spin webs in different shapes, and some do not spin webs at all.
13. a

Mitten Mix-up, page 171

Lost in Space, pages 172–173

1. G
2. C
3. F
4. B
5. D
6. E
7. A

Off the Deep End, pages 174–175

1. c
2. **True.** It won the unfortunate award in 2013.
3. a
4. d
5. b
6. **True.** The weird phenomenon is called a "brinicle," a combination of "brine" and "icicle."
7. c
8. a
9. b
10. c
11. b

What in the World? Global Gobbling, page 176

Top row: **Belgian waffles, Italian ice, Swedish meatballs**
Middle row: **Cuban sandwich, Brazil nuts, Greek salad**
Bottom row: **Brussels sprouts, English muffin, pad Thai**
Bonus: **a well-balanced meal**

Bizarre Laboratory Tale, pages 178–179

1. bunny lugs trophy
2. bear leaks tea
3. baby lifts tuba
4. bulldog loves troll
5. batter licks turkey
6. black belt lights torch
7. beaver locks tiger
8. boxer loses tic-tac-toe
9. ballerina lassos Tut
10. bride leads twins

Pet Project, page 182

What in the World? Aloha Spirit, page 183

Top row: **pineapples, leis, coconut**
Middle row: **Hawaiian shirt, hula dancer doll, sea turtle**
Bottom row: **volcano, surfboard, ukulele**

ANSWERS

In Your Backyard, pages 184–185

1. **c**
2. **False.** Dragonflies' eyes occupy most of their heads, so they can see in all directions except directly behind their heads.
3. **True.** Ladybugs can have stripes, spots, or no markings at all.
4. **a**
5. **c**
6. **c**
7. **b**
8. **d**
9. **d**
10. **True.** Earthworms eat as they burrow, consuming leaves, roots, and other decomposing matter in the soil.
11. **True.** A cockroach does not bleed to death when its head is cut off. Instead the blood clots at the neck, and the bug continues to breathe through little holes in its neck called spiracles. Cockroaches have been known to live for weeks without their heads.
12. **True, although it's very difficult.** The sidewalk would have to reach well over 150ºF (66ºC).
13. **d**
14. **b**

Go Fish! page 187

By the Numbers, pages 188–189

1. **c**
2. **b**
3. **b**
4. **b**
5. **b**
6. **c**
7. **d**
8. **True.** On the previous $100 bill, the time was 4:10. There's no historical significance to either time.
9. **d**
10. **d**
11. **c**
12. **c**

What in the World? Orange Overload, page 192

Top row: **basketball, tiger, carrots**
Middle row: **leaves, orangutan, monarch butterfly**
Bottom row: **pumpkin, cantaloupe, goldfish**
Bonus: **Sep-timber**

Animal Jam, Jammin' Jamaa, page 193

Cool Caves, pages 194–195

1. **d**
2. **b**
3. **a**
4. **False.** Bats sleep and live in many different places in addition to caves, including forests, cliffs, and buildings.
5. **d**
6. **a**
7. **a**
8. **a**
9. **a**
10. **b**
11. **d**
12. **a**
13. **b**
14. **d**

Book 'Em! page 196

Happy Holidays! pages 198–199

1. **False.** Chinese New Year can take place in January or February, because it's based on the Chinese, or Yin, calendar.
2. **a**
3. **True.** At the annual Monkey Buffet Festival, the people of Lopburi, Thailand, honor 2,000 long-tailed macaques that live nearby. Locals believe the monkeys bring good fortune.
4. **d**
5. **c**
6. **False.** A shamrock is a three-leaf clover, a shape often worn as a symbol of Ireland. A four-leaf clover is said to bring good luck.
7. **d**
8. **a**
9. **a**
10. **a**
11. **d**
12. **c**
13. **c**
14. **d**

339

Animal Games,
page 201

1. **golf course**
2. **pool**
3. **boxing ring**
4. **running track**
5. **bike track**
6. **badminton court**
7. **basketball court**
8. **fencing venue**
9. **rings**
10. **weight-lifting area**

Pocket Pets,
pages 202–203

1. **b**
2. **d**
3. **True.** The biggest this species from northern Africa gets is 3 inches (8 cm) long.
4. **a**
5. **c**
6. **True.** These fuzzy pets can jump over 6 feet (1.8 m), and some pet chinchillas have jumped on top of their owners' refrigerators!
7. **c**
8. **d.** Humans domesticated the guinea pig about 3,000 years ago.
9. **d**
10. **d**
11. **b**
12. **True.** There are African, Asian, and Indian varieties, all living in arid habitats.

What in the World?
Color Your World,
page 204

Top row: **sweaters, rainbow, sprinkles**
Middle row: **colored pencils, umbrella, toothbrushes**
Bottom row: **licorice, towels, feathers**
Bonus: **a pot of gold**

Ski Patrol,
page 205

Eat My Words!
pages 208–209

1. **a**
2. **b**
3. **a**
4. **b**
5. **d**
6. **False.** The classic tale by Judi Barrett takes place in a tiny town called Chewandswallow.
7. **True.** The French stew ratatouille is usually made with tomatoes, garlic, onions, zucchini, eggplant, peppers, and a mixture of tasty herbs.
8. **d**
9. **d**
10. **c**
11. **False.** She gives Edmund his favorite food, a sweet treat known as Turkish Delight.

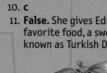

Out of This World,
pages 210–211

1. **c**
2. **b**
3. **d**
4. **a**
5. **d**
6. **b**
7. **a**
8. **c**
9. **False.** A water bag inside the space suit has a tube that goes inside the helmet so the astronaut can drink water.
10. **True.** A space walk usually lasts more than six hours, so the astronauts need this protection.
11. **d**

What in the World?
Below Sea Level,
page 213

Top row: **sea stars, octopus, seahorse**
Middle row: **angelfish, stingray, sea slug**
Bottom row: **blowfish, sea urchin, lobster**
Bonus: **sea cucumber**

DragonVille,
pages 214–215

1. **d**
2. **a**
3. **c**
4. **b**
5. **b**
6. **c**
7. **True.** Viking sailors were superstitious but not stupid; they took the dragon heads down as they approached land so they wouldn't frighten everybody else!
8. **d**
9. **a**
10. **c**
11. **False.** This line, which Bilbo Baggins says to himself, is quoted from J.R.R. Tolkien's book *The Hobbit.*
12. **b**
13. **False.** Barney is a large purple dinosaur that stars

in the children's television program *Barney & Friends*.

A-*maze*-ing Paris, pages 218–219

Name That Animal! page 221

1. **tiger shark**
2. **spider monkey**
3. **bullfrog**
4. **zebra fish**
5. **elephant seal**

Valentine Surprise, page 222

1. **Two peas in a pod.**
2. **We'll be together.**
3. **Be mine.**
4. **I'm nuts for you.**
5. **You and me are meant to be.**
6. **I adore you.**
7. **You rock.**
8. **Let us be buds.**
9. **You're one in a million.**

Find the Hidden Animals, page 223

1. **F**
2. **E**
3. **D**
4. **A**
5. **C**
6. **B**

Amazing Antarctica, pages 224–225

1. **d**
2. **b**
3. **True.** The average wind speed is 50 miles an hour (80 km/h).
4. **b**
5. **b**
6. **False.** Antarctica is a continent with no countries. The land has been managed under an international treaty since 1959. Today, 50 countries are part of the treaty.
7. **c**
8. **b**
9. **c**
10. **False.** In fact, more than 60 species of insects live in Antarctica.
11. **d**
12. **a**

Monster Maze, page 226

Change of Heart, page 228

Signs of the Times, page 229

Signs **1** and **6** are fake.

341

Aquarium Antics, pages 230–231

1. a
2. d
3. c
4. **True.** Angelfish can become quite aggressive and have been known to eat such aquarium mates as neon tetra fish.
5. c
6. b
7. c

8. **True.** The tank measures 26 feet (8 m) long and is about 100 times bigger than an average 10-gallon (38-L) tank.
9. a
10. a
11. b
12. a

In *Plane* Sight, page 272

Galaxy Quest, pages 234–235

What in the World? Face-to-Face, page 238

Top row: **shopping bag, chest of drawers, wall socket**
Middle row: **flower, fishing hat, cardboard box**
Bottom row: **cup lid, marble cake, mop**

Going Ape, pages 240–241

1. **True.** A gorilla's nose leaves a unique print.
2. **d**
3. **b**
4. **False.** Gorillas are mainly herbivores, eating fruit, leaves, seeds, and stems of plants.
5. **b**
6. **True.** Scientists have seen gorillas use tools, including sticks, to test the depth of streams.
7. **a**
8. **c**
9. True. Gorillas and adult humans have 32 teeth.
10. **a**
11. **a**
12. **b**
13. **c**

Noun Town, page 242

The 12 compound nouns are:
1. **sleeping bag**
2. **eggplant**
3. **catfish**
4. **bellhop**
5. **ladybug**

6. **housework**
7. **butterfly**
8. **limelight**
9. **arrowhead**
10. **full moon**
11. **sunflower**
12. **coffee table**

What in the World? X Marks the Spot, page 243

Top row: **calendar, train track, tic-tac-toe**
Middle row: **swimsuit, spider, roller coaster**
Bottom row: **windmill, pirate flag, satellite**
Bonus: **a slowpoke**

Undersea Stars, pages 245

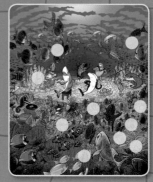

What in the World? The Sunshine State, page 247

Top row: **beach chair, conch shell, flip-flops**
Middle row: **palm tree, alligator, oranges**
Bottom row: **kite, wave, flamingo**
Bonus: **a Florida key**

ANSWERS

A Starry Show, pages 248–249

1. a
2. c
3. b
4. b
5. **False.** We see different constellations from Earth during different times of the year due to Earth's position in its orbit around the sun.
6. b
7. **True.** The constellation called Orion, the hunter, gets its name from Greek mythology.
8. d
9. a
10. **False.** Stars can only be seen through a clear sky with few or no clouds.
11. d
12. b
13. d
14. a

Teeing Off, page 250

From top to bottom, left to right: **Taj Mahal, towel, tent, Tower of Pisa, train tracks, train, totem pole, trash can, toolbox, T-shirt, trombone, tie, tables, tacos, tomatoes, telephone booth, teddy bear, trampoline, "The End" sign, tongue, truck, tires, tickets, toucan, teeth, turtle, tulips, trees, tennis racket, tees**

Map Mania! Fields of Dreams, pages 252–253

1. a
2. d
3. **True.** Each of the four screens on the video board is 72 feet high (22 m) and 160 feet wide (49 m), making for one heavy scoreboard!
4. c
5. a
6. d
7. b
8. Ski Dubai, **C—Dubai, United Arab Emirates**
9. Roman Colosseum, **A—Rome, Italy**
10. Cowboys Stadium, **G—Dallas, Texas, U.S.A.**
11. Wimbledon, **F—London, England**
12. Stadio Hernando Siles, **D—La Paz, Bolivia**
13. Rungrado May Day Stadium, **B—Pyongyang, North Korea**
14. Churchill Downs, **E—Louisville, Kentucky, U.S.A.**

Going Global, page 254

The ten things named after countries (and one continent) from around the world are: **the Chinese checkers, the African elephant lamp, the Swiss cheese, the Belgian waffle, the Scottish terrier, the French horn, the Canadian geese painting, the German shepherd, the Russian nesting dolls, and the Panama hat**

Picture-Perfect Fun Park, pages 256–257

What in the World? Go Undercover! page 258

Top row: **macaw, clam, crocodile**
Middle row: **jaguar, butterfly, zebra**
Bottom row: **red snapper, giraffe, chameleon**

Animal Groupies, pages 260–261

1. c
2. c
3. a
4. b
5. a
6. **True.** A group of crows can be called a murder or a flock.
7. b
8. **False.** Walruses live together in herds or pods. A group of lions is called a pride.
9. d
10. a
11. d
12. **True.** A group of goldfish can be called a troubling, a school, or a glint.
13. a
14. c
15. b

Just Desserts, pages 264–265

1. **True.** The ancient Olmecs, who lived in the southern Gulf of Mexico between 1200 B.C. and 400 B.C., made chocolate from cacao beans.
2. **b**
3. **c**
4. **c**
5. **True.** They were made from honey, flour, cheese, and olive oil.
6. **False.** Although pumpkins may have been present at the first Thanksgiving, sugar and ingredients for crust were not, so there was no pumpkin pie.
7. **b**
8. **True.** The recipe for "some mores" was published in a Girl Scouts cookbook in 1927. No one knows when the name of the treat was shortened to "s'mores."
9. **b**
10. **b**
11. **c**
12. **c**
13. **True.** Gingerbread houses were created in the 1800s after the Brothers Grimm described a house made of candy and cake in Hansel and Gretel.

Animal Jam, Awesome Autumn, page 266

Wild Guess! page 267

1. An adult *T. rex* stood up to 20 feet (6.1 m) tall; adult giraffes stand up to 19 feet (5.8 m) tall.
2. Riding the 8,133-foot (2,479-m)-long Steel Dragon roller coaster in Japan takes 3 minutes 40 seconds; microwave popcorn cooks for an average of two to three minutes.
3. The Leaning Tower of Pisa weighs about 31.9 million pounds (14,469,600 kg); the space shuttle weighs about 4.4 million pounds (1,995,800 kg).
4. Thunder can be heard up to 12 miles (19 km) away; a lion's roar can be heard 5 miles (8 km) away.
5. The fastest baseball pitch reached 107.9 miles an hour (173.6 km/h); the fastest racehorse ran 45 miles an hour (72.4 km/h).
6. California is 158,706 square miles (411,047 sq km); Italy is 116,000 square miles (300,439 sq km).

Hidden Hike, page 268

School Daze, page 269

What in the World? Purple Pizzazz, page 272

Top row: **daisy, plums, yarn**
Middle row: **glitter, sea star, mushroom**
Bottom row: **jellyfish, calculator, amethyst**
Bonus: **It ran out of juice.**

Bowling Freeze-Frame, page 273

1. **baboon fries fish**
2. **boy films frog**
3. **bowler feeds ferret**
4. **bulldog frees fairy**
5. **bicyclist finds fortune**
6. **bees frighten family**
7. **baker fans feet**

Coast to Coast, pages 274–275

1. **c**
2. **True.** The first horses arrived in Australia in 1788 by boat with the first Irish and British settlers.
3. **b**
4. **c**
5. **a**
6. **False.** Sand dunes are made up of loose sand formed into mounds by the wind, and are found in deserts, on beaches, and even on Mars!
7. **True.** The appearance of a sea cliff depends on the kind of rock that makes up

the wall. Some cliffs have rounded domes while others form more jagged edges.

8. **b**
9. **b**
10. **b**
11. **False.** Scientists estimate that there are about ten times more stars in the sky than grains of sand on Earth, including all the sand in deserts and on beaches!
12. **c**
13. **c**
14. **True.** The length of Canada's coastline is over 124,000 miles (200,000 km). How long is Poland's coastline? It's 273.4 miles (440 km).
15. **d**

What in the World? Hot and Cold, page 277

Top row: **ice cream, sun, snowy creek**
Middle row: **lava, frozen fruit, stove burner**
Bottom row: **glacier, chili peppers, ice rink**
Bonus: **a cold beard**

Game On! page 278

Name That Animal, page 280

1. **D**
2. **H**
3. **J**
4. **C**
5. **E**
6. **I**
7. **B**
8. **G**
9. **F**
10. **A**

Map Mania! Going Wild! pages 282–283

1. **North America**
2. **South America**
3. **Antarctica**
4. **South America**
5. **Antarctica**
6. **Europe**
7. **Asia**
8. **Australia and Oceania**
9. **Africa**
10. **Australia**
11. **Africa**
12. **Asia**

Surprises in the Teachers' Lounge, page 284

1. **E**
2. **A**
3. **I**
4. **J**
5. **H**
6. **C**
7. **D**
8. **F**
9. **G**
10. **B**

Let's Talk Turkey! page 287

1. **Swiss cheese**
2. **Belgian waffles**
3. **Italian ice**
4. **brussels sprouts**
5. **Philadelphia cheesesteak**
6. **English muffins**
7. **bologna**
8. **french fries**
9. **Canadian bacon**
10. **Danish pastry**
11. **New York cheesecake**
12. **buffalo wings**

Gear and Garb, pages 288–289

1. **b**
2. **a**
3. **True.** Goalies wear and use additional pads and equipment for protection and performance when playing "between the pipes."
4. **a**
5. **d**
6. **c**
7. **c**
8. **b**
9. **True.** In 1929, both the St. Louis Cardinals and New York Yankees placed numbers on the backs of their players to correspond to the order in which they batted.
10. **d**
11. **c**

Alive in the Rain Forest, pages 292–293

1. **b**
2. **True.** Orangutans have an arm span of some seven feet (2.1 m), which they rely on to swing through the treetops.
3. **b**
4. **d**
5. **b**
6. **d**
7. **True.** Amazon River dolphins range from gray to bright pink, depending on the clarity of the water. The darker the water, the pinker the dolphin.
8. **d**
9. **b**
10. **a**
11. **d**
12. **d**

A Piece of Cake, page 294

From left to right, top to bottom: **boy, birthday cake, bulldog, bicycle, bubbles, bread, barrel, ball, broom, beret, book, bear, belt, buns, ballerina, balloons, box, bow tie, bones, basket, buttons, bagels, baker, bowl, butter**

The Celebrity Scoop, pages 296–297

1. **a**
2. **b**
3. **c**
4. **True.** Cedric Diggory died in *The Goblet of Fire*.
5. **a**
6. **b**
7. **c**
8. **b**
9. **a**
10. **b**
11. **c**
12. **b**

Riddle Me This, page 298

1. *sneak*-ers, **2.** zebra,
3. tree, **4.** rain, **5.** candle,
6. footsteps, **7.** clock,
8. goose, **9.** bottle,
10. window.

Plant Party, pages 300–301

1. **c**
2. **True.** In Zimbabwe, an ancient baobab tree is large enough to contain 40 people inside its hollow trunk!
3. **b**
4. **a**
5. **c**
6. **b**
7. **b**
8. **True.** The mushroom known as the truffle can cost between $800 and $1,500 per pound!
9. **c**
10. **False.** Unripe green tomatoes are eaten by lots of people.
11. **d**

Eyes on the Prize, page 302

Music to Your Ears, pages 304–305

1. **b**
2. **d**
3. **c**
4. **True.** Before moving to Hollywood to become pop stars, the boys were lacing up their skates in Minnesota.
5. **b**
6. **c**
7. **d**
8. **False.** Adam Levine is the lead singer of Maroon 5.
9. **b**
10. **d**
11. **a**
12. **a**

Game On! pages 308–309

1. **c**
2. **a**
3. **b**
4. **d**
5. **c**
6. **a**
7. **c**
8. **False.** The object of *Tetris* is to make horizontal rows using different shapes as they fall.
9. **d**
10. **a-f, b-g, c-h, d-e**
11. **b**
12. **d**
13. **a**
14. **d**

What in the World? Wild Design, page 311

Top row: **giraffe, peacock, Dalmatian**
Middle row: **zebra, tiger, lionfish**
Bottom row: **tortoise, python, leopard**
Bonus: **natural camouflage**

ANSWERS

Roman Holiday, page 312

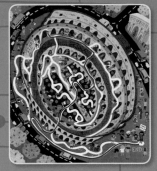

Think Fast! pages 314–315

1. c
2. b
3. b
4. d
5. c
6. a
7. a
8. **True.** The crew of the Apollo 10 spacecraft reentered Earth's atmosphere at this speed.
9. c
10. b
11. d

Birthday Bash! page 316

Animal Jam, It's a Jungle Out There! pages 318–319

Fashion Forward, pages 320–321

1. c
2. d
3. d
4. b
5. a
6. **False.** All Roman citizens were required to wear togas to gladiatorial games, weddings, and official ceremonies.
7. c
8. d
9. c
10. **True.** The wigs are used only during important ceremonies today.
11. c
12. a

We Gave It a Swirl, page 323

1. toucan
2. polar bear
3. sea star
4. zebra
5. sea lion

Color Café, page 324

Signs of the Times, page 325

Signs **2** and **4** are fake.

Incredible Inventions, pages 326–327

1. b
2. **True.** In 1905, 11-year-old Frank Epperson left a cup on his porch that was filled with powdered soda, water, and a stirring stick. It froze overnight. The next morning, Frank had discovered what would later become known as the Popsicle.
3. **True.** The ringtone, called "The Mosquito," is set at a higher frequency that only people under 25 years old can hear.
4. d
5. d
6. c
7. d
8. b
9. b
10. d
11. c
12. b
13. **False.** The fortune cookie was most likely invented in Japan and brought to the United States by immigrants.

CREDITS

Cover (UPRT), © istockphoto/mevans; cover (UPLE), Eric Isselee/Shutterstock; cover (CTR), prapass/Shutterstock; back cover (UPLE), Steve Bower/Shutterstock; back cover (UPRT), AnetaPics/Shutterstock; 1 (UP), Eric Isselee/Shutterstock; 1 (UP), Eric Isselee/Shutterstock; 3, prapass/Shutterstock; 7 (UP), © Suzi Eszterhas/Minden Pictures; 7 (CTR LE), © Exactostock/Superstock; 7 (CTR RT), © Fotosearch/Superstock; 7 (LO), © Stephen Dalton/NHPA/Photoshot; 7 (LO), © Stephen Dalton/NHPA/Photoshot; 8-9, Shutterstock/clearviewstock; 10 (UP), © Jason Gallier/Alamy; 10 (CTR), Jeffrey Hamilton/Getty Images; 10 (LO), © Tim Davis/Corbis; 12-13 (LOLE), Alexander Ishchenko/Shutterstock; 14-15, Shutterstock/kropic1; 15 (BACK), Kristin J. Mosher; 15, foryouinf/Shutterstock; 16, Stocksnapper/Shutterstock; 18, Eric Isselee/Shutterstock Inc.; 19 (UPLE), © Klein-Hubert/Kimball Stock; 19 (UP CTR), © Kenneth W. Fink/Ardea; 19 (UPRT), © Exactostock/SuperStock; 19 (CTR LE), © Martin Harvey/Corbis; 19 (CTR), © Joe & Mary Ann McDonald/Kimball Stock; 19 (CTR RT), © Klein-Hubert/Kimball Stock; 19 (LOLE), © AlaskaStock/Corbis; 19 (LORT), © Labat-Rouquette/Kimball Stock; 19 (LO CTR), © Javarman/Dreamstime; 20 (BACK), Kristin J Mosher; 20-21, Getty Images/Lonely Planet Images; 22 (UPRT), Kennan Harvey/Getty Images; 22 (LORT), Richard Newstead/Getty Images; 22 (CTR), Grant Dixon/Lonely Planet Images; 22 (UP CTR LE), Holger Leue/Lonely Planet Images; 22 (UPLE), Tony Anderson/Getty Images; 22 (LOLE), Alaska Stock Images/National Geographic Stock; 22 (LO CTR RT), Holger Leue/Lonely Planet Images; 23, Steven Hunt/The Image Bank/Getty Images; 24 (UP), S. Remain/Matton Images; 24 (LO), S. Remain/Matton Images; 26 (UP), Emjaysea/Dreamstime; 26 (LOLE), Smit/Shutterstock; 26 (RT), Pichugin Dmitry/Shutterstock; 27 (UP), Martin Maun/Shutterstock; 27 (CTR), EpicStockMedia/Shutterstock; 27 (LO), gary yim/Shutterstock; 28 (UP), ROY TOFT/National Geographic Image Collection; 28 (CTR LE), David Young-Wolff/Getty Images; 28 (CTR RT), © Sarah M. Golonka/Brand X Pictures/Jupiterimages; 28 (LO), © John Block/FoodPix/Jupiterimages; 30 (UPRT), © Free Agents Limited/Corbis; 30 (LOLE), © Ablestock/JupiterImages; 30 (UPLE), Hulton Archive/FPG/Getty Images; 30 (LO CTR RT), Shuji Kobayashi/Getty Images; 30 (LORT), Courtesy of Wilbur Street Paws Sphynx Cattery; 30 (UP CTR RT), State Fair of Texas; 31 (BACK), Kristin J. Mosher; 31 (CTR RT), Image Source/PictureQuest; 31 (LO CTR), Steven Mark Needham/FoodPix; 31 (UP CTR), Art Wolfe/Getty Images; 31 (UPRT), Derek P Redfearn/Getty Images; 31 (LOLE), Taxi/Getty Images; 31 (CTR), Rosemary Calvert/Getty Images; 31 (UPLE), Rebecca Hale/NGS Staff; 31 (CTR LE), © Photri/Ann & Rob Simpson; 31 (CTR), © Ron Kimball Studios; 32 (UP), Rudolf Tepfenhart/Shutterstock; 32 (CTR), Celso Diniz/Dreamstime; 32 (LOLE), Samot/Shutterstock; 32 (LORT), holbox/Shutterstock; 33 (UP), itsskin/iStockphoto; 33 (LOLE), Luis Marden/National Geographic Stock;33 (LORT), Tanawat Likitkererat/National Geographic My Shot/National Geographic Stock; 34 (UP), Steve Bower/Shutterstock; 34 (CTR LE), Fer Gregory/Shutterstock; 34 (CTR RT), © Akihito Yokoyama/Alamy; 34 (LOLE), Andrei Shumskiy/Shutterstock; 34 (LORT), Anastasios Kandris/Shutterstock; 34 (LO), moneymaker11/Shutterstock; 34 (LORT), Eric Isselee/Shutterstock; 36-37 (BACK), Kristin J. Mosher; 37 (UP CTR), Linas Lebeliunas/Dreamstime; 37 (LOLE), © Judith Collins/Alamy; 37 (LORT), Stuart Hunter/GettyImages; 37 (LO CTR), © Casey Edwards; 37 (CTR LE), JulNichols/iStockphoto; 37 (UPRT), artemisphoto/Shutterstock; 37 (UPLE), Robert Kyllo/Shutterstock; 37 (CTR RT), justasc/Shutterstock; 37 (CTR), © Cliff Hide Stock/Alamy; 38-39, debr22pics/Shutterstock; 40 (UPLE), © Amy Planz/Dreamstime; 40 (UP CTR), © Rafael Angel Irusta Machin/Dreamstime; 40 (UPRT), © Dulsita/Dreamstime; 40 (CTR LE), © Anke Van Wyk/Dreamstime; 40 (CTR), © Monkey Business Images/Dreamstime; 40 (CTR RT), © Marco Clarizia/Dreamstime; 40 (LOLE), © Dreamstime Agency/Dreamstime; 40 (LO CTR), © Sauletas/Dreamstime; 40 (LORT), © Matt Baker/Dreamstime; 42 (UP), Frank Lukasseck/Getty Images; 42 (LO), Frank Lukasseck/Getty Images; 43 (UP), © LYNN M. STONE/Nature Picture Library; 43 (CTR RT), Bradley Mason/Getty Images; 43 (CTR LE), © Konrad Wothe/Nature Picture Library; 43 (LO), © S & D & K Maslowski/Minden Pictures; 44 (LOLE), Catherine Lane/iStockphoto.com; 44 (CTR), © Lightzoom/Dreamstime.com; 44 (UPLE), © skodonnell/iPhotostock.com; 44 (UPRT), © David Brabiner/Alamy; 45 (LO), © martin lauricella/Alamy; 45 (UPRT), © Franck Fotos/Alamy; 46 (UPLE), © Bob Barbour/Minden Pictures; 46 (UP CTR), © pepebouza/Alamy; 46 (UPRT), Jamie Grill/Aurora Photos; 46 (CTR LE), © Larry Brownstein—Rainbow/Science Faction/Corbis; 46 (CTR), © Don Hadden/ardea; 46 (CTR RT), © Ross Hoddinott/Nature Picture Library; 46 (LOLE), Christophe Launay/Aurora Open/Aurora Photos; 46 (LO CTR), © Metta foto/Alamy; 46 (LORT), © BeachShooter/Alamy; 47 (BACK), Kristin J. Mosher; 48 (UP CTR), © Stockbyte/PictureQuest; 48 (CTR LE), © Howard Davies/Corbis; 48 (UPRT), © Pat O'Hara/Corbis; 48 (UPLE), © Julie Habel/Corbis; 48 (LORT), © David Keaton/Corbis; 48 (LOLE), © Dale O'Dell/Corbis; 48 (CTR RT), © Joseph Sohm/PictureQuest; 50-51, © Hinrich Baesemann/dpa/Corbis; 50-51 (BACK), Kristin J. Mosher; 52 (UPLE), © Cao Hai/Dreamstime; 52 (UP CTR), © Khunaspix/Dreamstime; 52 (UPRT), © Laurel Stewart/Dreamstime; 52 (CTR LE), © WaterFrame/Alamy; 52 (CTR), © Sim Kay Seng/Dreamstime; 52 (CTR RT), © Mark Bowler/Alamy; 52 (LORT), © estancabigas/Alamy; 52 (LO CTR), © Suzi Eszterhas/Corbis; 52 (LOLE), Alistair Michael Thomas/Shutterstock; 53 (UPLE), Gerry Ellis/Minden Pictures/National Geographic Stock; 53 (CTR LE), © Thomas Dressler/Getty Images; 53 (UPRT), © Piotr Naskrecki/Minden Pictures; 53 (LORT), Biosphoto/Juan-Carlos Muñoz; 53 (LOLE), © Piotr Naskrecki/Minden Pictures; 53 (CTR RT), © Valerie Taylor/Ardea; 54 (LORT), alslutsky/Shutterstock; 54 (UPLE), Mitsuhiko Imamori/Minden Pictures/Corbis; 54 (UPRT), Dani Vincek/Shutterstock; 55 (LORT), Claudio Divizia/Shutterstock; 55 (UPRT), Moviestore collection Ltd/Alamy; 57, Mark Thiessen, NGP; 58-59, Jagronick/Dreamstime; 60 (UPLE), Mark Harwood/Getty Images; 60 (UP CTR), Wilfried Krecichwost/Getty Images; 60 (UPRT), Foodcollection RF/Getty Images; 60 (CTR LE), © Steven Mark Needham/Envision/Corbis; 60 (LO CTR), Joel Sartore/National Geographic Stock; 60 (UPRT), Ken Lucas/Visuals Unlimited, Inc./Getty Images; 60 (LOLE), © Radius Images/Alamy; 60 (LO CTR), Sandy Jones/Getty Images; 60 (LORT), © Michael & Patricia Fogden/Minden Pictures; 61 (UPRT), © PhotoObjects.net/Jupiterimages; 61 (UPLE), Kate Fredriksen/Shutterstock; 61 (LOLE), Niki Crucillo/Shutterstock; 61 (UPLORT), Eric Isselee/Shutterstock; 61 (LO CTR), AlexKol Photography/Shutterstock; 61 (UPRT), Danny Smythe/Shutterstock; 62 (UPLE), Vulnificans/Dreamstime; 62 (CTR), Lobacheveb/Dreamstime; 62 (LO-B), Dave_cgn/Dreamstime; 62 (LO-C), Richard Hermann/Visuals Unlimited, Inc./Getty Images; 62 (LO-D), Joop Snijder Jr./Shutterstock; 62 (LO-A), Erik Mandre/Dreamstime; 63 (UP), Ahmad Faizal Yahya/Shutterstock; 63 (LO), ManoAfrica/iStockphoto; 64 (UPLE), © Gavril Margittai/Dreamstime; 64 (UP CTR), © Dhilde/Dreamstime; 64 (UPRT), © Nilanjan Bhattacharya/Dreamstime; 64 (CTR LE), © Sue Daly/Nature Picture Library; 64 (CTR), © Steve Stedman/Dreamstime; 64 (CTR RT), Mauricio Handler/National Geographic Creative; 64 (LOLE), © iStock/aimintang; 64 (LO CTR), © Bhalchandra Pujari/Dreamstime; 64 (LORT), © Flyver/Alamy; 65 (UP), © David Aubrey/Corbis; 65 (CTR RT), © Larry Lilac/Alamy; 65 (CTR LE), GK Hart/Vikki Hart/Getty Images; 65 (CTR LE), Stockbyte/Getty Images; 66 (LOLE), American Broadcasting Companies, Inc.; 66 (UPRT), © AF archive/Alamy; 66 (CTR RT), © AF archive/Alamy; 67 (LORT), 2012 Cindy Ord/Getty Images; 67 (LOLE), Moviestore collection Ltd/Alamy; 68-69 (LOLE), Alexander Ishchenko/Shutterstock; 69 (BACK), Kristin J. Mosher; 69, David Evison/Shutterstock Inc.; 70-71, Dioscoro L. Dioticio/Shutterstock; 72-73, Eric Isselee/Shutterstock Inc.; 75 (BACK), Kristin J. Mosher; 75 (UP), © Ingo Arndt/Minden Pictures; 75 (CTR RT), Diane Collins and Jordan Hollender/Getty Images; 75 (LO), Thorsten Milse/Getty Images; 75 (CTR LE), © Dreammasterphotographer/Dreamstime; 76 (UPLE), © Brandon Alms/Dreamstime; 76 (UPLE), © Bidouze Stéphane/Dreamstime; 76 (UPRT), © Natakuzmina/Dreamstime; 76 (CTR), © Tamara Kulikova/Dreamstime; 76 (CTR), © Hotshotsworldwide/Dreamstime; 76 (CTR RT), © Sergey Galushko/Dreamstime; 76 (LOLE), © Brian Grant/Dreamstime; 76 (CTR LE), © Ammit/Dreamstime; 76 (LORT), © Ika66/Dreamstime; 76 (CTR LE), © Ammit/Dreamstime; 77 (RT), © Eric Isselée/Shutterstock; 77 (LE), © vitor costa/Shutterstock; 77 (LORT), © Ronen/Shutterstock; 77 (UPRT), © Viorel Sima/Shutterstock; 77 (LOLE), © Ah Teng/Shutterstock; 78-79 (BACK), Kristin J. Mosher; 78-79, Shutterstock/Petrenko Andriy; 80 (LOLE), © Ron Kimball Studios; 80 (UP CTR), © Henry Diltz/Corbis; 80 (UP CTR), Amy White And Al Petteway/National Geographic Image Collection; 80 (LOLE), © Wolfgang Kaehler/Corbis; 81 (LO CTR), © Ron Kimball Studios; 81 (CTR RT), © Creatas/PictureQuest; 81 (LORT), © Royalty-Free/Corbis; 81 (UPRT), © Royalty-Free/Corbis; 81 (UPLE), Johnny Johnson/Getty Images; 81 (UPRT), © Marc Chamberlain/Seapics.com; 81 (LORT), Paul Souders/Getty Images; 81 (RT CTR), Tim Laman/National Geographic Image Collection; 81 (LO), © Gary Bell/Corbis; 81 (UPLE), Photodisc Green/Getty Images; 83 (UPRT), jollyphoto/iStockphoto; 84 (UP), lucafabbian/iStockphoto; 84 (LOLE), DNY59/iStockphoto; 84 (RT), Kristin Smith/Shutterstock; 85 (UP), inkit/iStockphoto; 85 (LO), HKPNC/iStockphoto; 86 (UPLE), © Jaynes Gallery/Danita Delimont; 86 (UP CTR), © Duncan Usher/Minden Pictures; 86 (UPRT), © Kristy-Anne Glubish/Design Pics/Corbis; 86 (CTR), © Lars Persson/Naturbild/Corbis; 86 (CTR), © Thomas Marent/Ardea; 86 (CTR RT), © Pauli Nieminen/plainpicture/Corbis; 86 (LOLE), © Pascal Goetgheluck/Ardea; 86 (LO CTR), © IndexStock/SuperStock; 86 (LORT), Danita Delimont/Getty Images; 87, © James Phelps Jr/Dreamstime; 88-89, Kristin J Mosher Images; 88-89 (BACK), Fer Gregory/Shutterstock; 90 (UP), Miroslav Hlavko/Shutterstock; 90 (LOLE), © Kameel/iStockphoto; 90 (UP), Eric Isselee/Shutterstock; 90 (CTR RT), Krzysztof Wiktor/Shutterstock; 93 (UPRT), © Dannyphoto80/Dreamstime; 93 (CTR LE), Marcin Pawinski/Dreamstime; 93 (UPLE), © Tonny Anwar/Dreamstime; 93 (LOLE), © Denis Nikitin/Dreamstime; 93 (CTR), © Daniel Prudek/Dreamstime; 93 (CTR RT), © Thi Thuy Anh Pham/Dreamstime; 93 (UPRT), © Jinfeng Zhang/Dreamstime; 93 (LO CTR), © Marcio Silva/iStockphoto; 93 (UP CTR), © Olena Chernenko/iStockphoto; 94-95, Worakit Sirijinda/Shutterstock; 96 (UPLE), © Gerry Ellis/Minden Pictures; 96 (UPRT), © Michael & Patricia Fogden/Minden Pictures; 96 (CTR RT), © Fred Bavendam/Minden Pictures; 96 (CTR RT), Julie Larsen Maher © Wildlife Conservation Society; 96 (LOLE), © Gary K. Smith/Minden Pictures; 96 (LORT), © Wild Wonders of Europe/Widstrand/Nature Picture Library; 97 (UPRT), © Gynane/Dreamstime; 97 (LORT), © Chris Dorney/Dreamstime; 97 (LOLE), © A.P.S. (UK)/Alamy; 97 (CTR RT), © Elena Elisseeva/Dreamstime; 97 (UP CTR), David Sanger/Getty Images; 97 (LO CTR), © Androniques/Dreamstime; 97 (CTR RT), © Travelling-light/Dreamstime; 97 (CTR RT), © Dambuster/Dreamstime; 97 (UPRT), JACK HILL/AFP/Getty Images; 100 (UPLE), © Lauri Patterson/iStockphoto.com; 100 (LORT), JeniFoto/

348

Shutterstock.com; 101 (UPLE), Goran Bogicevic/Shutterstock.com; 101 (CTR RT), Nikin7d/Shutterstock.com; 101 (LOLE), Shutterstock/Zastolskiy Victor; 102, © Pavel German; 103 (UPLE), © Ferrero-Labat/ardea; 103 (UP CTR), Fuse/Getty Images; 103 (UPRT), Still Images/Getty Images; 103 (CTR LE), Steve McAlister/Getty Images; 103 (CTR), © Juniors Bildarchiv/Alamy; 103 (CTR RT), © Glow Images/SuperStock; 103 (LOLE), Win Initiative/Getty Images; 103 (LO CTR), © Friedrich Von Horsten/Animals Animals—Earth Scenes, All rights reserved; 103 (LORT), © Birgitte Wilms/Minden Pictures; 104 (UP), Apic/Getty Images; 104 (CTR), PictureLake/iStockphoto; 104 (LO), rook76/Shutterstock; 105 (UPLE), Neftali/Shutterstock; 105 (LE ctr), traveler1116/iStockphoto; 105 (UPRT), Bettmann/Corbis; 105 (LO), ©Warner Brothers/Everett Collection, Inc.; 108 (UPLE), cbpix/Shutterstock; 108 (UPRT), Christian Musat/Shutterstock; 108 (LOLE), Nagy Melinda/Shutterstock; 108 (RT CTR), FloridaStock/Shutterstock; 108 (LORT), Christian Musat/Shutterstock; 109 (UPLE), © Roberto A Sanchez/iStockphoto.com; 110, Kellie L. Folkerts/Shutterstock Inc.; 112 (LOLE), Shutterstock/Yuri Kravchenko; 112 (UPRT), Shutterstock/kyokoliberty; 113 (LOLE), Shutterstock/WOLF AVNI; 113 (UPRT), Taylor Hill/Getty Images; 115 (UPRT), © Donald M. Jones/Minden Pictures; 115 (CTR RT), © Grafner/Dreamstime; 115 (CTR LE), © Dreammasterphotographer/Dreamstime; 115 (LORT), ILYA AKINSHIN/Shutterstock; 115 (LORT), © PetStockBoys/Alamy; 116-117, marco_tb/Shutterstock; 118 (UPLE), © Pablo631/Dreamstime; 118 (UP CTR), © Eyewave/Dreamstime; 118 (UPRT), © Christian Bridgwater/Dreamstime; 118 (CTR LE), © Yin Jian Ng/Dreamstime; 118 (CTR), © Tombaky/Dreamstime; 118 (CTR RT), © Eutoch/Dreamstime; 118 (LOLE), © Giuseppe Ramos/Dreamstime; 118 (LO CTR), © Mihail Orlov/Dreamstime; 118 (LORT), © Chris Wood/Dreamstime; 119, karamysh/Shutterstock Inc.; 122 (CTR RT), StudioSmart/Shutterstock; 122 (LOLE), MartiniDry/Shutterstock; 122 (LORT), Shutterstock/Katstudio; 122 (CTR LE), Shutterstock/S_E; 122 (CTR LE), Graeme Dawes/Shutterstock.com; 123 (UPRT), KirVKV/iStockphoto.com; 123 (LOLE), Shutterstock/Sumikophoto; 123 (LO CTR), © EduardHarkonen/iPhotostock.com; 123 (LORT), Shutterstock/Sergey Peterman; 123 (CTR RT), joppo/Shutterstock; 123 (UP CTR), extradeda/Shutterstock.com; 124 (UP), © Jurgen & Christine Sohns/Minden Pictures; 124 (CTR LE), © Iulian Gherghel/Dreamstime; 124 (CTR LE), Mike Flippo/Shutterstock; 124 (CTR RT), Pixsooz/Shutterstock; 124 (LO), Andrey_Kuzmin/Shutterstock; 124 (LO), Valentyn Volkov/Shutterstock; 126-127, Triff/Shutterstock; 128 (UPLE), © Ron Sumners/Dreamstime; 128 (UP CTR), © Chrisp543/Dreamstime; 128 (UPRT), © Elf0724/Dreamstime; 128 (CTR LE), © Hanhanpeggy/Dreamstime; 128 (CTR), © Imaengine/Dreamstime; 128 (CTR RT), © Anthony Baggett/Dreamstime; 128 (LOLE), © Alexey Stiop/Dreamstime; 128 (LO CTR), © Saiko3p/Dreamstime; 128 (LORT), © Pius Lee/Dreamstime; 128-129, Shutterstock/kitty; 129, Shchipkova Elena/Shutterstock; 130, Mark Thiessen, NGP; 131, Jim Paillot; 134-135, Speedfighter17/Dreamstime; 136 (UPRT), AR Images/Shutterstock Inc.; 136, Eric Isselée/Shutterstock; 137 (LOLE), © Suzi Eszterhas/Minden Pictures; 137 (LORT), © Sharon Dominick; 137 (LOLE), © Matteo photos/Shutterstock; 137 (UPLE), © Johan Swanepoel/Shutterstock; 139, mountainpix/Shutterstock; 140-141, Shutterstock/YK; 142 (UPLE), Yuji Sakai/Getty Images; 142 (UP CTR), Roman Sigaev/Shutterstock; 142 (UPRT), © MIMAGES/Alamy; 142 (CTR LE), Loskutnikov/Shutterstock; 142 (CTR), © Pablo Scapinachis/Dreamstime; 142 (CTR RT), Ira Heuvelman-Dobrolyubova/Getty Images; 142 (LOLE), Pressmaster/Shutterstock; 142 (LO CTR), © Ron Sumners/Dreamstime; 142 (LORT), © Samantha Carrirolo/Getty Images; 143, Nagel Photography/Shutterstock Inc.; 146-147, Yuri Arcurs/Shutterstock; 149 (UPRT), Kitchin & Hurst/leesonphoto; 149 (CTR LE), © William Joseph Boch Photography/StockFood; 149 (CTR LE), Joel Sartore/National Geographic Stock; 149 (CTR RT), © Tony Savino/Corbis; 149 (LO), © Photo Op/StockFood; 150-151, Eric Isselee/Shutterstock; 152-153, Lambros Kazan/Shutterstock; 154 (LOLE), gualtiero boffi/Shutterstock Inc.; 154 (LOLE), MilousSK/Shutterstock Inc.; 154 (UPLE), © Teeratas/Shutterstock; 154 (UPLE), © Esterio/Dreamstime; 154 (LORT), © Hannamariah/Shutterstock; 154 (UPLE), © Tomica Ristic/Shutterstock; 156 (UPRT), wynnter/iStockphoto; 156 (LOLE), joecicak/iStockphoto; 157 (UPLE), Chip Somodevilla/Getty Images; 157 (LE CTR), Oleg Golovnev/Shutterstock; 157 (lo), Sarah Dreyer/Dreamstime; 158 (UPRT), Kesu/Shutterstock; 158 (UP CTR), Stubblefield Photography/Shutterstock; 158 (UPRT), Phoric/Shutterstock; 158 (LE CTR), Robert Marien/Corbis; 158 (CTR), Studio Araminta/Shutterstock; 158 (RT CTR), Fedor Selivanov/Shutterstock; 158 (LOLE), Joel Sartore/NationalGeographicStock.com; 158 (LO CTR), Blaz Kure/Shutterstock; 158 (LORT), Eric Isselée/Shutterstock; 159, HPH Image Library/Shutterstock; 160 (UPRT), Chester Tugwell/Shutterstock.com; 160 (UPLE), Iakov Kalinin/Shutterstock.com; 160 (LOLE), Pius Lee/Shutterstock.com; 160 (LORT), nmiskovic/Shutterstock.com; 161 (UPRT), Vladitto/Shutterstock.com; 161 (CTR RT), Hung Chung Chih/Shutterstock.com; 161 (LORT), Dan Breckwoldt/Shutterstock.com; 162 (UPRT), Laborant/Shutterstock; 162 (LORT), Kalmatsuy/Shutterstock; 162 (UPLE), Mircea Bezergheanu/Shutterstock; 163, Reinhold Leitner/Shutterstock; 164 (LORT), Stephen Frink/Getty Images; 164 (LOLE), Accent Alaska/Alamy; 164 (LO CTR), Frans Lanting/National Geographic Stock; 164 (UP), Philip Game/Getty Images; 165 (UP), David Keaton/Corbis; 165 (CTR), Quinn Rooney/Getty Images; 165 (LO), Tui De Roy/Minden Pictures; 166 (UPLE), © Image Source/Corbis; 166 (UP CTR), Jeffrey Coolidge/Getty Images; 166 (UPRT), © Stock Connection/Superstock; 166 (CTR LE), © Superstock; 166 (CTR), © Sergio Pitamitz/Corbis; 166 (CTR RT), Neal Mishler/Getty Images; 166 (LOLE), © Corbis/Superstock; 166 (LO CTR), AP Photo/U.S. Mint; 166 (LORT), © Exactostock/Superstock; 167, Smart Bomb Interactive; 168-169, wong yu liang/Shutterstock; 170 (UPRT), © Superstock; 170 (UPRT), © Superstock RF; 170 (LOLE), Waku/Shutterstock Inc.; 174 (UPLE), Caters News Agency/Newscom; 174 (LORT), 2013 Imeh Akpanudosen/Getty Images; 175 (UPRT), Wong Hock weng/Shutterstock.com; 175 (LORT), bluehand/Shutterstock.com; 176 (UPLE), Marie C. Fields/Shutterstock; 176 (UP CTR), © liv friis-larsen/Alamy; 176 (UPRT), Robyn Mackenzie/Shutterstock; 176 (CTR LE), REDAV/Shutterstock; 176 (CTR), Discovod/Shutterstock; 176 (CTR RT), © Mirceax/Dreamstime; 176 (LOLE), © Jale Evsen Duran/Dreamstime; 176 (LO CTR), © Svetlana Foote/Dreamstime; 176 (LORT), Andrea Skjold/Shutterstock; 177, © Sergemi/Dreamstime; 180-181, irin-k/Shutterstock; 182, Pat Moriarty; 183 (UPLE), Eising FoodPhotography/StockFood; 183 (UP CTR), Craig Aurness/Veer/Corbis; 183 (UPRT), BananaStock/Jupiter Images; 183 (CTR LE), BananaStock/Jupiter Images; 183 (CTR), PhotoObjects.net/Jupiter Images; 183 (CTR RT), Stephen Frink Collection/Alamy; 183 (LOLE), James L. Amos/NationalGeographicStock.com; 183 (LO CTR), Douglas Peebles/eStock Photo; 183 (LORT), Siede Preis/Getty Images; 184 (LOLE), Denis Tabler/Shutterstock; 184-185 (BACK), Nejron Photo/Shutterstock; 185 (LO), 4FR/Shutterstock; 186 (UPRT), © Jim Cornfield/Corbis; 186 (UPLE), Carsten Reisinger/Shutterstock; 186 (LO), Mark Herreid/Shutterstock; 188 (UPRT), © Pictorial Press Ltd/Alamy; 188 (CTR LE), Shutterstock/Nomad_Soul; 188 (LORT), Shutterstock/Pablo Rogat; 189 (UPRT), Shutterstock/Welland Lau; 189 (CTR RT), Shutterstock/images.etc; 189 (CTR RT), Shutterstock/Dimedrol68; 189 (LORT), Shutterstock/Tatiana Popova; 190-191, szefei/Shutterstock; 192 (UPLE), © Michael Flippo/Dreamstime; 192 (UP CTR), © Ketian Chen/Dreamstime; 192 (UPRT), © Wimstime/Dreamstime; 192 (LO CTR), © Liz Van Steenburgh/Dreamstime; 192 (CTR), © Ronald Van Der Beek/Dreamstime; 192 (CTR LE), Poznyakov/Shutterstock; 192 (CTR RT), © Davidcrehner/Dreamstime; 192 (LOLE), © Melissa Connors/Dreamstime; 192 (LORT), manley099/iStockphoto; 194-195 (BACK), Marcos Casiano/Dreamstime; 197 (UPRT), Jagodka/Shutterstock; 197 (LO), Apples Eyes Studio/Shutterstock; 198-199 (LO), kamisoka/iStockphoto; 198 (UPLE), Vakhrushev Pavel/Shutterstock; 200 (UPRT), © Elvele Images Ltd/Alamy; 200 (UPRT), © Pioneer111/Dreamstime; 200 (UPLE), © Alaska Stock/Alamy; 200 (LO), Yakovleva Zinaida Vasilevna/Shutterstock; 202 (LORT), Shutterstock/Eric Isselee; 202 (CTR LE), Shutterstock/margouillat photo; 202 (UPRT), Shutterstock/Lepas; 203 (LORT), Shutterstock/Eric Isselee; 203 (UPLE), Shutterstock/vovan; 204 (UPLE), © Pavel Losevsky/Dreamstime; 204 (UP CTR), © Chris Hill/Dreamstime; 204 (UPRT), © Barbara Helgason/Dreamstime; 204 (CTR LE), © Grigor Atanasov/Dreamstime; 204 (CTR), © Darak77/Dreamstime; 204 (CTR RT), © Micha360/Dreamstime; 204 (LOLE), © Brad Calkins/Dreamstime; 204 (LO CTR), © Gary Arbach/Dreamstime; 204 (LORT), © Vasily Kovalev/Dreamstime; 205, James Yamasaki; 206 (BACK), Pakhnyushchy/Shutterstock; 206 (LOLE), Danny Smythe/Shutterstock; 206 (LE CTR), irin-k/Shutterstock; 207 (UPRT), Comstock/Getty Images; 207 (LOLE), Aleksei Verhovski/Shutterstock; 207 (LORT), Eric Isselee/Shutterstock; 207 (LO CTR RT), RTimages/Shutterstock; 207 (UPLE), Eric Isselee/Shutterstock; 208 (UPLE), Shutterstock/Maks Narodenko; 208 (CTR RT), Shutterstock/urbanlight; 208 (LORT), © huronphoto/iStockphoto.com; 209 (UPRT), © AF archive/Alamy; 209 (CTR LE), Shutterstock/Tlaszlo; 210-211, Getty Images/Science Faction; 212, Winfried Wisniewski/Minden Pictures; 213 (UPLE), © Junda/Dreamstime; 213 (UP CTR), © Planctonvideo/Dreamstime; 213 (UPRT), © Hannu Viitanen/Dreamstime; 213 (CTR LE), © Mayama/Dreamstime; 213 (CTR), © Annette Boettcher/Dreamstime; 213 (CTR RT), © Kelpfish/Dreamstime; 213 (LOLE), © Ernst Daniel Scheffler/Dreamstime; 213 (LO CTR), © Derek Holzapfel/Dreamstime; 213 (LORT), © John Anderson/Dreamstime; 214-215, Mariusz S. Jurgielewicz/Shutterstock; 216, David Courtenay/Getty Images; 217 (UPRT), © Steve Bloom Images/Alamy; 217 (LOLE), Erik Lam/Shutterstock Inc.; 217 (CTR RT), Kraska/Shutterstock Inc.; 218-219, CTON; 220 (BACK), Nicemonkey/Shutterstock; 220 (CTR), Jacob Hamblin/Shutterstock; 221,; 223 (UP CTR), © Visuals Unlimited/Corbis; 223 (CTR RT), © DLILLC/Corbis; 223 (CTR LE), © W. Perry Conway/Corbis; 223 (UPRT), © Donald M. Jones/Minden Pictures; 223 (LOLE), © Thomas Rabeil/Nature Picture Library; 223 (LORT), © Fred Bavendam/Minden Pictures; 224 (LOLE), imagebroker.net/SuperStock; 224 (UPLE), Dmytro Pylypenko/Alamy; 224 (UPRT), Dan Leeth/Alamy; 225 (RT), Jan Martin Will/Shutterstock; 225 (LE), Pan Xunbin/Shutterstock; 226, James Yamasaki; 227 (UPRT), Peter Dazeley/Getty Images; 227 (UPLE), Paul Burley Photography/Getty Images; 227 (LO), topseller/Shutterstock; 228, Clayton Hanmer; 229 (CTR LE), Rick Strange/Index Stock Imagery; 229 (CTR), © Royalty-Free/Corbis; 229 (LOLE), © Annie Griffiths Belt/Corbis; 229 (LORT), Doug Plummer/Getty Images; 229 (UP CTR RT), © Layne Kennedy/Corbis; 229 (LO CTR RT), © Roger Wood/Corbis; 229 (UPRT), Matthias Clamer/Getty Images; 230 (LOLE), Shutterstock/Photobank gallery; 230 (CTR RT), Shutterstock/serg_dibrova; 230 (UPLE), Shutterstock/Michaelboyer91; 230 (UPRT), Shutterstock/Mariusz Niedzwiedzki; 231 (LOLE), Shutterstock/bluehand; 231 (CTR RT), Shutterstock/bluehand; 232, Brian Lasenby/Shutterstock Inc.; 234-235 (D), Clayton Hanmer; 236 (LE), panbazil/Shutterstock; 236 (CTR), terekhov igor/Shutterstock; 236 (LO CTR inset), Leemage/Universal Images Group/Getty Images; 236 (LORT inset), The Granger Collection, NYC—All rights reserved; 236 (LO CTR), Iakov/Shutterstock; 236 (LORT), Nina Malyna/Shutterstock; 237, panbazil/Shutterstock; 237 (LOLE inset), The Bridgeman Art Library/Getty Images; 237 (UPRT), Nikreates/Alamy; 237 (RT CTR), The Bridgeman Art Library/Getty Images; 237 (LORT inset), Pool Photograph/Corbis; 237 (LORT), Ninell/Shutterstock; 238 (UP), Travel Inc/Getty Images; 239 (UPRT), Geoff Dann/Getty Images; 239 (UPRT), © Tim Zurawski/Dreamstime; 239 (LO CTR), Shukaylova Zinaida/Shutterstock; 239 (LORT), Maximus256/Shutterstock; 239 (LO CTR), Vitalii HulaiShutterstock; 239 (UPLE), Joe Belanger/Shutterstock; 239 (CTR LE), AlexKZ/Shutterstock; 239 (UP), Three Lions/Getty Images; 240-241, Thomas David Pinzer/Alamy; 240, Chris Jackson/Staff/Getty Images; 241 (LO), Russell Kord/Alamy; 241 (LO), Russell Kord/Alamy; 241 (UPLE), AP Images/

Adrian Wyld/The Canadian Press; 241 (UPRT), Chris Wattie/Reuters/Corbis; 241 (LORT), Howard Sandler/Shutterstock; 242.; 242 (A), CP Photo/Irma Coucill/Canadian Press Images; 242 (B), CP Photo/Irma Coucill/Canadian Press Images; 242 ©, CP Photo/Irma Coucill/Canadian Press Images; 242 (E), CP Photo/Irma Coucill/Canadian Press Images; 242 (F), CP Photo/Irma Coucill/Canadian Press Images; 242 (G), CP Photo/Irma Coucill/Canadian Press Images; 242., 243 (UPLE), Simon Battensby/Getty Images; 243 (UP CTR), © drmadra/iStockphoto; 243 (UPRT), © vtaner/iStockphoto; 243 (CTR LE), Nilsson, Huett, Ulf/Getty Images; 243 (CTR), © Tim Gainey/Alamy; 243 (CTR RT), © Zoe Mack/Alamy; 243 (LORT), VICTOR HABBICK VISIONS/Getty Images; 243 (LO CTR), © ManuelVelasco/iStockphoto; 243 (LOLE), compassandcamera/iStockphoto; 243 (A), CP Photo/Irma Coucill/Canadian Press Images; 243 (B), CP Photo/Irma Coucill/Canadian Press Images; 243 ©, CP Photo/Irma Coucill/Canadian Press Images; 243 (D), CP Photo/Irma Coucill/Canadian Press Images; 243 (F), CP Photo/Irma Coucill/Canadian Press Images; 243 (G), CP Photo/Irma Coucill/Canadian Press Images; 243 (H), CP Photo/Irma Coucill/Canadian Press Images; 243 (J), CP Photo/Irma Coucill/Canadian Press Images; 243.; 243.; 244, Audrey Snider-Bell/Shutterstock; 244 (A), CP Photo/Irma Coucill/Canadian Press Images; 244 ©, CP Photo/Irma Coucill/Canadian Press Images; 244 (D), CP Photo/Irma Coucill/Canadian Press Images; 244 (E), CP Photo/Irma Coucill/Canadian Press Images; 244 (F), CP Photo/Irma Coucill/Canadian Press Images; 244 (G), CP Photo/Irma Coucill/Canadian Press Images; 244 (I), CP Photo/Irma Coucill/Canadian Press Images; 244 (J), CP Photo/Irma Coucill/Canadian Press Images; 244.; 245.; 245.; 246 (LOLE), saddako/Shutterstock Inc.; 246 (UPRT), maminez/Shutterstock Inc.; 246 (LORT), Jag_cz/Shutterstock Inc.; 246 (CTR RT), Andy Dean Photography/Shutterstock Inc.; 246 (LORT), © gibsons/Shutterstock; 246 (LORT), © Peter Blazek/Shutterstock; 246, Universal History Archive/Contributor/Getty Images; 246, Brownstock/Alamy; 247 (UPLE), © Tanawat Pontchour/Dreamstime; 247 (UP CTR), © Beata Becla/Dreamstime; 247 (UPRT), © Sofiaworld/Dreamstime; 247 (CTR LE), © Czalewski/Dreamstime; 247 (CTR), LaDora Sims/Getty Images; 247 (CTR RT), © Agustua Fajarmon/Dreamstime; 247 (LOLE), © Rosario Manzo/Dreamstime; 247 (LO CTR), © Jinyoung Lee/Dreamstime; 247 (LORT), © Eleden/Dreamstime; 247.; 247.; 248-249, Jamen Percy/Shutterstock; 248 (BACK), John E. Marriott/All Canadian Photos/Getty Images; 248 (INSET), Rolf Hickler/All Canadian Photos/Getty Images; 249, Thomas Marent/Minden Pictures; 249 (UPLE), Wayne R. Bilenduke/Stone/Getty Images; 249 (LORT), Norbert Rosing/National Geographic Creative; 250, CTON; 250 (UP), Glenbow Archives NA-2204-5; 251 (LO), Marco Mayer/Shutterstock; 251 (UP), Maggie/Shutterstock; 251 (UPLE), imging/Shutterstock; 251 (UPLE), Richard Lautens/Toronto Star/ZUMA Press/Newscom; 251 (UPRT), Bill Becker/Canadian Press Images; 251 (LORT), Adrien Veczan/Canadian Press Images; 252 (LORT), Shutterstock/Ken Durden; 252 (LOLE), Shutterstock/tkachuk; 252 (CTR), © Vladimir Zhuravlev/Dreamstime; 253 (UPLE), © trentham/Dreamstime.com; 253 (CTR), Dmitry Burlakov/Shutterstock.com; 253 (LOLE), © Laura Stone/Dreamstime.com; 253 (LO CTR RT), © Kevin R. Morris/Corbis; 255 (UPLE), Oleg Kozlov/Shutterstock; 255 (UPRT), © Stan Fellerman/Alamy; 255 (CTR RT), © Photos.com/Jupiterimages; 255 (LOLE), © FoodCollection/StockFood; 256-257, James Yamasaki; 258 (CTR), © Gavriel Jecan/Corbis; 258 (LORT), Art Wolfe/Getty Images; 258 (LO CTR), © Tory Lepp/Corbis; 258 (UP), Stephen St. John/National Geographic Image Collection; 258 (UPRT), Steve Taylor/Getty Images; 258 (CTR LE), John Cancalosi/Peter Arnold, INC.; 258 (CTR RT), Digital Vision/Getty Images; 258 (UP CTR), © Doug Perrine/SeaPics.com; 258 (UPRT), © Buddy Mays/Corbis; 259, David Kossheck/Shutterstock Inc.; 259, Maks Narodenko/Shutterstock Inc.; 259 (UPLORT), Vitaly Titov & Maria Sidelnikova/Shutterstock; 260-261, António Jorge Da Silva Nunes/Dreamstime; 262, Volodymyr Burdiak/Shutterstock Inc.; 262, Elena Schweitzer/SHutterstock Inc.; 263, Michel Cecconi/Shutterstock Inc.; 263, Dmitry Kalinovsky/Shutterstock Inc.; 263, Petr Malyshev/Shutterstock Inc.; 263, Iryna Rasko/Shutterstock Inc.; 263, Phillip W. Kirkland/Shutterstock Inc.; 263, zirconicusso/Shutterstock Inc.; 264 (UP), Dio5050/Dreamstime; 264 (CTR), Elena Elisseeva/Shutterstock; 264 (LOLE), 4kodiak/iStockphoto; 265 (UP), beusbeus/iStockphoto; 265 (RT CTR), Ildi Papp/Shutterstock; 265 (LOLE), jenjen42/iStockphoto; 267 (a), Roy Toft/NationalGeographicStock; 267 (b), Jim Zuckerman/Corbis; 267 (a), GWImages/Shutterstock; 267 (b), Toru Yamanaka/AFT/Getty Images; 267 (a), NASA; 267 (b), Corbis; 267 (A), Kristian Sekulic/Shutterstock; 267 (b), Jhaz Photography/Shutterstock; 267 (a), Shutterstock; 267 (b), Stephen Mcsweeny/Shutterstock; 269, Clayton Manmer; 270-271, Tony Campbell/Shutterstock Inc.; 272 (UPLE), Purestock/Getty Images; 272 (UP CTR), Ken Lucas/Visuals Unlimited, Inc./Getty Images; 272 (UPRT), © Ingram Publishing/Superstock; 272 (CTR LE), © Duffie/Alamy; 272 (CTR), © Fred Bavendam/Minden Pictures; 272 (CTR RT), photontrappist/Getty Images; 272 (LOLE), © Chris Newbert/Minden Pictures; 272 (LO CTR), © Sheli Spring Saldana/Dreamstime; 272 (LORT), Dorling Kindersley/Getty Images; 272 (CTR), © Fred Bavendam/Minden Pictures; 273, Pat Moriarity; 274-275, Khoroshunova Olga/Shutterstock; 276, TRyburn/Shutterstock; 277 (CTR LE), © Jason Yoder/Dreamstime; 277 (LOLE), © Pablo Caridad/Dreamstime; 277 (UP CTR), © Serban Enache/Dreamstime; 277 (CTR), © Alena Brozova/Dreamstime; 277 (CTR RT), © Brad Calkins/Dreamstime; 277 (UPLE), © Dmitry Ternovoy/Dreamstime; 277 (UPRT), © Ventura69/Dreamstime; 277 (LO CTR), © Vitaly Korovin/Dreamstime; 277 (LORT), © Lorraine Swanson/Dreamstime; 279 (UPRT), © William Mullins/Alamy; 279 (CTR LE), © Arindom Chowdhury/Dreamstime; 279 (CTR RT), M. Unal Ozmen/Shutterstock; 279 (LORT), © Vilainecrevette/Dreamstime; 280 (UPLE), © Digital Vision/Punchstock; 280 (UPLE), © Jerry Shulman/SuperStock; 280 (LORT), © L. Johnson; 280 (UPRT), © Stockbyte/Punchstock; 280 (CTR RT), © Mark Raycroft/Minden Pictures; 280 (UP CTR LE), © Ulrike Schanz/Animals Animals; 280 (CTR), DAJ/Getty Images; 280 (LO CTR LE), © Wegner/ARCO/Nature Picture Library; 280 (LOLE), © Mark Raycroft/Minden Pictures; 280 (LO CTR), © L. Johnson; 281 (LORT), Martin Lukasiewicz/NationalGeographicStock.com; 281 (UPRT), Aliakseyenka Mikita/Shutterstock Inc.; 281 (CTR LE), Stone/Getty Images; 281 (CTR RT), Cameron Watson/Shutterstock; 282 (1), B & T Media Group Inc./Shutterstock; 282 (2), Thomas Marent/Minden Pictures/National Geographic Stock; 282 (3), Achim Baque/Shutterstock; 282 (4), Cuson/Shutterstock; 282 (5), Stormcastle/Dreamstime; 282 (6), Angel Sosa/Dreamstime; 283 (9), Andy Rouse/Getty Images; 283 (7), Gerry Ellis/Digital Visions; 283 (8), Tom McHugh/Getty Images; 283 (10), Jan Pokorn/Dreamstime; 283 (11), Steve Allen/Dreamstime; 283 (12), Anan Kaewkhammul/Shutterstock; 285 (UPRT), © Guido Vrola/Dreamstime; 285 (LOLE), © Maisna/Shutterstock; 285 (LORT), © Kathy Burns-Millyard/Shutterstock; 285 (LOLE), © RubberBall/Superstock; 285 (LOLE), © ALEAIMAGE/iStockphoto; 286, canoniroff/Shutterstock; 288 (UPLE), Brocreative/Shutterstock.com; 288 (CTR RT), miqu77/Shutterstock.com; 288 (CTR LE), Michael Pettigrew/Shutterstock; 288 (LO), Shutterstock/homydesign; 289 (UPRT), Andresr/Shutterstock; 289 (CTR LE), Aspen Photo/Shutterstock; 290-291, Vasyl Helevachuk/Shutterstock; 293 (LO), Lusoimages/Shutterstock; 294, Aaron Reiner; 295 (BACK), © Elena Blokhina/Shutterstock; 295 (LORT), © Toy boat in waterpool/Shutterstock; 295 (LOLE), © Kamenetskiy Konstantin/Shutterstock; 295 (UPLE), © Graham Stewart/Shutterstock; 295 (LO), Warren Goldswain/Shutterstock; 296 (UP), sonny2962/iStockphoto; 296 (LOLE), Aaron Settipane/Dreamstime; 296 (LORT), Denis Makarenko/Dreamstime; 297 (UP), Featureflash/Shutterstock; 297 (LO), SteveChristensen/iStockphoto; 299 (UPRT), © Booka/Shutterstock; 299 (UPRT), Szasz-Fabian Ilka Erika/Shutterstock; 299 (BACK), © gibsons/Shutterstock; 299 (UPLE), © Peter Blazek/Shutterstock; 299 (LO), an Rentoul/Shutterstock; 299 (CTR LE), Richard Peterson/Shutterstock; 300-301, Cathy Keifer/Shutterstock.com; 303, Giancarlo Liguori/Shutterstock Inc.; 304-305 (UP), XiXinXing/Shutterstock; 306-307, Eric Isselee/Shutterstock; 308-309 (BACK), Athanasia Nomikou/Shutterstock; 310, Michio Hoshino/Minden Pictures; 311 (UPLE), © Karin Van Ijzendoorn/Dreamstime.com; 311 (UP CTR), © Vladislav Turchenko/Dreamstime.com; 311 (UPRT), © Andreas Gradin/Dreamstime.com; 311 (CTR LE), © Alexey Petrunin/Dreamstime.com; 311 (LO CTR), © Yairleibovich/Dreamstime.com; 311 (CTR RT), © Chai117/Dreamstime.com; 311 (LOLE), © Dannyphoto80/Dreamstime.com; 311 (LORT), © Isselee/Dreamstime.com; 311 (LORT), © Lubo Chlubn/Dreamstime.com; 313 (LORT), © W. Scott/Shutterstock; 313 (LORT), © ene/Shutterstock; 313, Pavel K/Shutterstock Inc.; 313, Grigory L/Shutterstock Inc.; 313, Grigory L/Shutterstock Inc.; 313, Symbiot/Shutterstock Inc.; 314 (UPRT), © Tim Laman/National Geographic Society/Corbis; 314 (UPLE), © Warren Wimmer/Icon SMI/Corbis; 314 (CTR RT), Shutterstock/Andre Coetzer; 314 (LORT), Shutterstock/Max Earey; 314 (LO CTR RT), Shutterstock/Darren Brode; 314 (LO CTR LE), © Car Culture/Corbis 60/Car Culture/Corbis; 314 (LOLE), Shutterstock/Darren Brode; 315 (UPRT), Shutterstock/javarman; 315 (LORT), Shutterstock/Anton Balazh; 317, Fotopic/Index Stock Imagery, Inc./Photolibrary.com; 318-319, Smart Bomb Interactive; 320 (UPLE), Eric Limon/Shutterstock.com; 320 (LORT), violetblue/Shutterstock.com; 320, Mike Theiss/National Geographic Society/Corbis; 320, JLR/Getty Images; 321 (LORT), © sarnadex/Shutterstock.com; 321 (LO CTR RT), Mike Flippo/Shutterstock.com; 321 (LO CTR LE), © Michael Flippo/Dreamstime.com; 321 (LOLE), © H. Armstrong Roberts/ClassicStock/Corbis; 321 (CTR RT), Hank Shiffman/Shutterstock.com; 321, Matejay/iStockphoto; 321, Flip Nicklin/Minden Pictures; 322, Joel Sartore; 322 (LOLE), © Pixel Embargo/Shutterstock; 322 (UPRT), © Sukharevskyy Dmytro (nevodka)/Shutterstock; 322 (UPRT), © Ber Lybil/Dreamstime; 322 (UPRT), Szasz-Fabian Ilka Erika/Shutterstock; 322, Rolf Hicker Photography/Getty Images; 322, Marina Jay/Shutterstock; 323 (CTR RT), © Exactostock/SuperStock; 323 (UPLE), Theo Allofs/Getty Images; 323 (UPRT), Nick Norman/National Geographic Stock; 323 (LOLE), © Natural Selection David Ponton/Design Pics/Corbis; 323 (LORT), © Kevin Schafer/Alamy; 323, Pete Ryan/Getty Images; 323, Rolf Hicker Photography/Alamy; 324, James Yamasaki; 324, John Alabaszowski/Contributor/Getty Images; 325 (UPRT), © Greg Elms/Lonely Planet Images; 325 (LO CTR RT), © Peter Ptschelinzew/Lonely Planet Images; 325 (UP CTR RT), © Richard Cummins/Lonely Planet Images; 325 (CTR), Jason Edwards/National Geographic Stock; 325 (CTR LE), Brian Summers/Getty Images; 325 (LORT), Joseph Sohm/Visions of America/Getty Images; 325 (LOLE), Wendy White/Hot Topic Images; 325, Barrett & MacKay/Getty Images; 326 (UPRT), Panoramic Images/Getty Images; 326 (UP CTR LE), TKTKTK; 326 (UP CTR RT), TKTKTKTK; 326, PhotoDisc; 326, blickwinkel/Alamy; 326, Mark Duffy/Alamy; 327-327, Kim Kyung-Hoon/Reuters/Corbis; 327, © Howiewu/Dreamstime.com; 327, © Chee-onn Leong/Dreamstime.com; 327, © Aivoges/Dreamstime.com; 327, © Alberto Dubini/Dreamstime.com; 327, © age fotostock/Alamy; 327 (UP CTR RT), BGSmith/Shutterstock; 327 (RT CTR), Biosphoto/SuperStock; 327 (LO CTR RT), Tom Vezo/Danita-Delimont.com; 327 (LORT), Barrett & MacKay/All Canada Photos/Corbis; 327, Steve Ogle/Getty Images; 329, Jorg Greuel/Photographer's Choice/Getty Images; 330-331, Max Sudakov/Shutterstock

Copyright © 2015 National Geographic Society

All rights reserved. Reproduction of the whole or any part of the contents without written permission from the publisher is prohibited.

Staff for this Book

Kate Olesin, *Project Editor*
Eva Absher-Schantz, *Art Director*
Lisa Jewell, *Photo Editor*
Ruthie Thompson, *Designer*
Carl Mehler, *Director of Maps*
Paige Towler, *Editorial Assistant*
Sanjida Rashid, *Design Production Assistant*
Colm McKeveny, *Rights Clearance Specialist*
Michael Cassady, *Rights Clearance Assistant*
Michael Libonati, *Special Projects Assistant*
Grace Hill, *Managing Editor*
Michael O'Connor, *Production Editor*
Lewis R. Bassford, *Production Manager*
Robert L. Barr, *Manager, Production Services*
Susan Borke, *Legal and Business Affairs*

Published by the National Geographic Society

Gary E. Knell, *President and CEO*
John M. Fahey, *Chairman of the Board*
Melina Gerosa Bellows, *Chief Education Officer*
Declan Moore, *Chief Media Officer*
Hector Sierra, *Senior Vice President
and General Manager, Book Division*

Senior Management Team, Kids Publishing and Media

Nancy Laties Feresten, *Senior Vice President*
Jennifer Emmett, *Vice President,
Editorial Director, Kids Books*
Julie Vosburgh Agnone, *Vice President,
Editorial Operations*
Rachel Buchholz, *Editor and Vice President,
NG Kids magazine*
Michelle Sullivan, *Vice President, Kids Digital*
Eva Absher-Schantz, *Design Director*
Jay Sumner, *Photo Director*
Hannah August, *Marketing Director*
R. Gary Colbert, *Production Director*

Digital

Anne McCormack, *Director*
Laura Goertzel, Sara Zeglin, *Producers*
Jed Winer, *Special Projects Assistant*
Emma Rigney, *Creative Producer*
Brian Ford, *Video Producer*
Bianca Bowman, *Assistant Producer*
Natalie Jones, *Senior Product Manager*

The National Geographic Society is one of the world's largest nonprofit scientific and educational organizations. Founded in 1888 to "increase and diffuse geographic knowledge," the Society's mission is to inspire people to care about the planet. It reaches more than 400 million people worldwide each month through its official journal, *National Geographic,* and other magazines; National Geographic Channel; television documentaries; music; radio; films; books; DVDs; maps; exhibitions; live events; school publishing programs; interactive media; and merchandise. National Geographic has funded more than 10,000 scientific research, conservation, and exploration projects and supports an education program promoting geographic literacy.

For more information, please visit nationalgeographic.com, call 1-800-NGS LINE (647 5463), or write to the following address:
National Geographic Society
1145 17th Street N.W.
Washington, D.C. 20036-4688 U.S.A.

Visit us online at
nationalgeographic.com/books

For librarians and teachers:
ngchildrensbooks.org

More for kids from National Geographic:
kids.nationalgeographic.com

For information about special discounts for bulk purchases, please contact National Geographic Books Special Sales: ngspecsales@ngs.org

For rights or permissions inquiries, please contact National Geographic Books Subsidiary Rights: ngbookrights@ngs.org

Trade paperback ISBN: 978-1-4263-2106-1

Printed in China
15/PPS/1

FUN IS IN, BOREDOM IS OUT!

Discover EVERYTHING about EVERYTHING in the world's most popular kids' almanac—jam-packed with photos, facts, and tons of fun!

NATIONAL GEOGRAPHIC KiDS

© 2015 National Geographic Society

Available Wherever Books Are Sold

Discover more FUN STUFF at kids.nationalgeographic.com